The Identity of God

THE SEARCH FOR AND IDENTIFICATION OF GOD
THROUGH ANCIENT TEXTS

By: Jeffery L. Sortino
Second Edition

Table of Contents

Dedication

I'd like to dedicate this book to my wife (Toni) and kids (Talia and Taran) who urged me to stop talking, (my wife would say lecturing) and start writing about all the knowledge I have acquired over the years.

This book is also dedicated to all truth seekers. I feel there are many out there that have a desire, but do not have the time to research. I have read all of the ancient books mentioned in this one book, but I have summarized, like cliff-notes, important parts that I have emphasized so that the readers could gain some knowledge without having to spend the time and effort researching everything I have. I hope this helps.

Chapter 1
<u>The Beginning of Critical Thinking</u>

      I could sense light, but my eyes were still shut. Barely coming to, I cracked one eye lid to confirm the light. Upon confirmation, I immediately shut that eyelid again. Yep, it was morning. Oh, I was so tired. Trying to ignore the sensation of light that I could detect through my closed eyelids, I turned my head to the other side away from the window where the sunshine was coming through. This made it a little darker and allowed me to relax a little more to continue sleeping. My bed was so comfortable and I did not want to get up now. I laid there for some time not really knowing for how long, but I knew it wasn't hours. Then, a thought came to my head as I laid there trying to stave off my awakening. Maybe it's early enough that some cartoons are on the television. Usually Saturdays and loaded with a line-up of cartoons all morning and just about every kid in America that had a TV longed for Saturday mornings. However, this was Sunday, but sometimes if you got up early enough there would be a couple of cartoon programs on before all the televangelists would take over the airwaves for their televised sermons.

      So, wondering if my stupid brother was already up before me, I proceeded to get up out of bed and walk into the hallway from my bedroom which immediately then entered the living room where the tv was turned off. It seemed I was the first one up this morning. Having to blink my eyes a couple times because my vision was still blurry, I focused on the clock on the wall. It was 6:05 am. I went over to the tv and turned it on. I turned the rotary dial on the tv to channel 3. Sure enough, a cartoon was on. Even though the time of the color television was mainstream, many shows in syndication were still in black and white. Woody Woodpecker was one of these shows and the cartoon that now was being received. I was happy, like any kid of my age would be for receiving my favorite type of candy on Halloween. Making sure that it wasn't too loud to wake my mom (I really didn't care if it waked my brother), I scooted back from the tv and plopped down on the couch. It was one of those couches that every household seemed to have in the 70's.

It had a wood frame with cushions that had a lot of off white, brown, beige, and rustic orange with designs of old western wagon wheels or steering wheels for navigation on old ships. The kind of colors you see a lot on Thanksgiving decorations. I was still in my "tidy whitey" underwear and no shirt. I always preferred to just wear underwear to bed instead of pajamas that I seemed to outgrow a couple years ago.

It wasn't long before my brother came out to the living room from his bedroom. Obviously, he must have heard the tv, because he looked like I did just a couple of minutes ago. Rubbing his eyes trying to clear his blurry vision and still in his "tidy whiteys", he staggered to where I was on the couch. I said, "What's up, dummy?" He retorted, "Shut up, Jeff." He then proceeded to pass me and plop down on the empty space beside me. Regardless of how mean it seemed I was to my brother, I actually loved him very much. Like many friends and close family, many people tend to use derogatory names towards one another, but really, they are terms of endearment. Only close friends or family could get away with speaking such names to each other and not arouse the anger in the one to whom they are speaking. I was 11 years old at the time and my brother Todd was 2 ½ years younger than me. It was just us two siblings. My mother and father had divorced 2 years prior and our custody was bestowed to my mother. My brother and I didn't know why they divorced, as I'm sure most kids did not understand these matters at such a young age and oblivious to even the idea of romantic relationships and the many variables that come with making a relationship work. We were now living in a three-bedroom apartment, which we were lucky to get, because somehow my mother was able to get this apartment for the same rent as a two bedroom. She was always able to procure the sympathy of others for her given situation. Sometimes it was warranted and sometimes it wasn't. My father was always an atheist and still is at the time I am writing this. He has always maintained that once you are dead, all that you become is 'worm food'. My mother, on the other hand, would be what I call a religious person, but not devout.

She always liked what Christianity taught as far as the good feeling she felt when the message was pushed for kindness to others, overall love, and the oneness of family. While going to church seemed important, at the same time, my mother has repeatedly said, "Well, you can't believe everything that's in the Bible." That phrase always stayed with me over the years as I grew up, knowing full well that my mother had never really read the Bible. However, all we knew right now is that Woody Woodpecker was on and we had a little time to watch tv before the boring televangelists came on.

The second half hour Woody Woodpecker episode was almost over when my mother's bedroom door opened and she came walking into the living room to see her two boys still in their underwear, sitting on the couch watching tv. She kind of giggled, shook her head, and walked into the kitchen to get a glass of milk. She was already dressed in some jeans and nice looking long sleeved black blouse with white floral designs on it. She was only 4'11" tall and I was starting to outgrow her at almost 12 years of age. As she poured the milk in a glass, she was telling us that we, too, should always get a glass instead of drinking out of the carton. I can remember being so scared with the refrigerator door open and thinking I could get a quick drink from the carton, when my mother had a knack for coming around the corner just as I was doing this. The hair on my neck and arms would stand on end and a not so pleasant tingling feeling would shoot down my spine as she would see and then subsequently yell at me for doing so. The fear would then heighten because you never knew when the yelling would be followed by a slap across the face, back of the head, or if you were lucky, you would catch it on the arm or shoulder. Depending on how angry she already was with me, my brother, or both, the slap would come with varying degrees of intensity and power. As she told us to always get a glass, we both responded, "Ok, mom!" She said after that cartoon we should start getting ready for church. We both let out a "Ahhh" in disappointment. We didn't go to church every week. It seemed we would go whenever my mother felt like it. Sometimes it was more consistent than other times, only on Sundays, of course. I asked, "Do we have to go to church mom?"

She responded by saying if I hurried, we could get there in time to have a couple donuts. That's all she had to say. She reminded us that there were donuts. Our eyes got big with the idea exploding in our head, "Oh yeah." We both fervently got up from the couch to go shower and get ready for church promptly after Woody Woodpecker was finished a couple minutes later. Just in time too. Before exiting the living room, I could see the introduction to the "700 Club" program came on tv. For those of you reading this that don't know, it was a popular televangelist program.

After getting ready for church, we all got into our one car mom had, a 1972 red ford pinto station wagon. It had ripped up seats, but enough cushion still inside the upholstery that it wasn't uncomfortable to sit on. My brother and I wore jeans (I had three pair, but only 1 pair without holes in them) and the best long-sleeved shirt we had, which happened to be a country type shirt not really meant for a tie. Todd and I both wore our tennis shoes of an off brand that were our only pair. We were an upper-lower class family when my parents were together, but now that they were divorced, my mother was on welfare and food stamps and worked as a barber (not a cosmetologist) cutting people's hair. My mother didn't have much of an education and the court system in that day wasn't as strict at enforcing child support laws. My brother and I really didn't understand how poor we were and how much my mother struggled to make ends meet. My mother thought it was really important to teach us about God and not to ever give up hope. I remember praying to God that we would be accepted for a new apartment or that my mom would be hired for a better job, or that my mom would just be happy when she was sad. I really don't remember a time when I didn't believe in God. I always have.............and I always kept praying.

Arriving at the church, we got out of the pinto and proceeded to the front door of the church. It was a small traditional style church with the steeple being toward the front of the building over the front entrance. There were approximately 10 rows of pews on either side of the main room.

Toward the back of the church was a raised platform about a foot higher than the floor where the pastor preached from. There was large wooden cross suspended behind the platform on the back wall. We lived in a small town in Ohio at this time (my mother later remarried a man in the military which kept us moving) and the church we went to was a local Lutheran church. We usually attended whatever protestant church was close to us. Growing up, we moved a lot and attended all sorts of denominations – Presbyterian, Lutheran, Baptist, Methodist, ect. With slight differences not apparent, they are all pretty much the same. My mother didn't trust the Catholic Church and thought of them as evil somehow by trying to control everybody. If you knew my mother, the one thing she couldn't stand is to have someone try to control her. This is one of the many reasons that lead to my parent's divorce. They both like to be in control of the relationship. I call them both, control freaks. (smiling) Being greeted by people at the front of the church we went into the lobby. My brother and I made a bee-line for the donuts. My mother always had to remind us not to take more than two each. Otherwise, being growing boys, we would probably eat them all. We would never make it early enough for Sunday school, nor would I want to go, so we always attended the service when mom went. The pastor's sermon was from Genesis. He was nice looking man. Clean shaven about 6 feet tall in his 40's. Although too long for a boy of my age, there were times that I was quite focused. This was one of those times. When the pastor continued, in _Genesis 1:26_ God said,

"Let US make Man in OUR image and after OUR likeness."

I thought to myself, wait a minute! If there is only one God, why does the Bible say that God made man in OUR image, meaning plural? It seemed to me that God was talking to others like himself. I later asked my mother about this, but because she never really read the Bible, she always deferred the question to a pastor or minister. That same question would arise again when the pastor would go over the 10 commandments. _Exodus 20:3_ - The very first commandment is:

"You shall not have any other Gods before me!"

I thought to myself. There it is again. By saying this, was God referring to others like him?

Later in life when I read Erik Von Danniken's book, "Chariots of the Gods" I realized that I wasn't the first to have this question. Whenever I would ask a pastor or someone that was supposedly more knowledgeable about scripture than others, when talking about the creation of Man, they would say that God was referring to the Holy Trinity (God the Father, God the Son, and God the Holy Spirit all being one). This did not make any sense to me. When expressing this later in life, the response was always, _it's not supposed to make sense. We are men, how are we supposed to understand the thinking of God? It is too_ *complex for us to understand. ....***OR***, there are just somethings Mankind was not meant to know!*

When referring to the first commandment, the explanation would be that people tend to love things over God, such as money, fame, vanity, power, ect. Giving these "things" a personification of Gods.   Time after time, explanation after explanation, throughout my life I never received an explanation that was satisfactory and made any sense.   So, my question about these scriptures continued.

When the service was over, we made our way to the front door shaking everybody's hand and telling them that it was good to see them. On the way home, my mother said, "Jeffy (to this day she still calls me Jeffy), are you feeling OK? You are especially quiet."   I nodded yes and kept looking out the window.   I was consumed in thought about the sermon and meaning of those scriptures.   I was trying to wrap my head around them.   I continued to do this throughout my life when given the explanations I mentioned above as well.

However, today was the start of me learning and the beginning of my critical thinking when it came to scripture and when it came to God.

Chapter 2

Having Faith

I felt the presence of someone in my room before I even opened my eyes. I was in my bed and someone had just shaken me. I awoke and looked up to a strange man above me standing next to my bed. He had a mustache and glasses and he was in a uniform. He was bathed in intermittent red and blue lights that were coming in from my window. It was still dark outside. I was puzzled and was trying to make sense of what was going on. At the same time, I noticed other people our apartment in the hallway while I heard screaming coming from my mother's room. My step father was in the Army and was overseas in Germany at the time. I soon realized that it was my mother's voice that was screaming. My brother Todd and I slept in the same bed the night before, because my mother had agreed to babysit a younger girl who was the daughter of a neighbor. The girl was sleeping in my brother's bedroom while he doubled up with me. I had just turned 15 and realized that the man that woke us up and the people in the hallway were paramedics and policemen. They rushed us past my mother's room and down the stairs to the exit. The red and blue lights bathed the entire complex in light that was coming from emergency vehicles parked in front. As I was rushed past my mother's room, I caught a glimpse of my mother naked on the floor sitting down with her back against the wall and pushing with her feet, but there was nowhere she could go. She had her hands out in front of her as if to guard against something and a dual purpose of gesturing not to come any closer. A female paramedic was inching closer to her with a covering of some sort, like they were trying to capture a dangerous animal. I stopped for a brief moment because I was worried about my mom, but I was pushed to keep going forward from the paramedics behind me. They tried to shield my eyes to what was going on in my mom's room. My mother looked like something was wrong with her and she had gone crazy. She would scream anytime someone came close to her. Her face was all black and blue. She had been beaten up pretty badly. Once downstairs, the police were "beating around the bush" about what happened, but I was able to ascertain what happened from their description.

My mother had been beaten and raped by an intruder who broke into our home by lifting the downstairs window screen and entering through a window. He had stayed most of the night and rested in between the sexual assaults while I and the other children slept. He raped her 3 times before departing before the sunrise.

His fingerprints were on the doorknob to my brother's bedroom where the little neighbor's girl had been sleeping, as well as, my room. The police said this showed that he opened both doors to check on us before closing them once again and entering my mother's bedroom. The little girl was not harmed. He placed a pillowcase over my mother's head and put a gun to it and told her that if she didn't do what he wanted, he was going to kill her kids. She wanted to fight back, but she did what she had to do to protect her children. She later told me that she prayed to God and had and out-of-body experience in order to endure the event. I remember praying to God to help her as we were being taken away by police to a shelter. I was numb to what was happening around me, because I felt helpless. Being 15 and my brother 12 1/2, I was almost a man; however, I was still a boy and I could not protect or help the people that I loved. Hearing my mother scream uncontrollably like that scared me to the bone. The guilt I felt not being able to stop what happened to my mother ate me up inside for many years to come. I prayed and prayed for my mother to be OK. They kept her for psychiatric evaluation, as well as, physical assessment for about a week while my brother and I stayed with my mother's female friend. It took many years of counseling and psychiatric care to get my mother to function in society without relapsing. A large part of who my mother was died with her that night. She was never quite the same again.   I was just thankful to God that she was alive. I also had a question for God. WHY? Why would God let this happen? If Satan is to blame for this, then WHY would God let him do this?

From age 12 through high school I was really a good-hearted kid that felt weak and vulnerable, probably because I couldn't do anything about the bad things that happened to my family in my life coupled with my stature.   I grew to be only 5'8" tall. That isn't an extremely short height, but I was always a late bloomer. I got bullied a lot and seemed to be scared of my own shadow anytime I had to stick up for myself. I remember one time in 9th grade on my first day at a new school after moving to a new state, sitting on the benches in the locker room during gym class. A group of about 5 boys lead by 1 really mean boy, started making fun of me. Looking for anything about me that he could to pick on.   Calling me ugly and that my face looked stupid. He started making fun of my clothes, because my family was poor and we did not have brand name clothes.   I was scared because I was cornered and couldn't run away. They took my lunch money for the cafeteria out of my pocket. I was too scared to defend against it. I went hungry a lot. I remember wishing I had something to eat. We had to take part in gym class, but I didn't have any gym clothes to change into, so the gym coach made me take part in activities anyway. When we were finished, the coach said that it was his policy that everyone must shower afterward. I told him that I didn't have any change of clothes or a towel. He told me that I would have to borrow a towel, but I still must take a shower.

I felt like it was my first day in an adult prison. (I am assuming that is what the fear would be like, never being in prison myself.)

I took the shower so I wouldn't get in trouble, but when I got back to my locker where I had undressed, my clothes were gone. Anybody I asked to use their towel told me NO! So, naked and wet, I went to the coach's office and told him what had happened. He yelled at me and said it wasn't his problem and that I should figure something out. There were 2 other coaches in his office and nobody said anything. I was even more scared now, because there was nobody to help me. This was the days before everybody had a cell phone. Fighting the feeling all this time, I now started to cry. I remember the feeling of despair. I picked up a wet towel that was on the floor that seemed to not belong to anybody. I dried off best I could and covered myself with it. The whole class left to go to their next class. I was left sitting on the bench were my clothes used to be. I had searched every locker I could to not avail. The next class was going to start soon and I was going to be tardy. The coach came out and yelled at me why I wasn't dressed. I reminded him that somebody had taken my clothes. He seemed upset at me more than the boys that did it. He stormed off out of the locker room without saying anything to me. I was miserable just waiting in the locker room, too scared and embarrassed to go into the hallway to try to find my clothes. I didn't know what I was going to do. I started praying to God to help me - to be with me so I wouldn't have this feeling of hopelessness. I really was a good kid with a kind heart and I never wanted to hurt anyone. After a few minutes, the coach came back in with my clothes. He set them down hard on the bench beside me and stormed off without an explanation. I still think he was mad at me. I felt so alone. I only had God to make me feel like I wasn't. Years later, I assumed the coach was thinking he wouldn't be doing me any favors if he coddled me. I guess his policy was one of "tough love". ......OR, he could have just been a jerk at a time when teachers and coaches were not kept accountable for their actions.

As a sophomore in high school, I started to play football and work out with weights always admiring the professional bodybuilders in Muscle & Fitness magazines. I still got bullied and was scared to death when someone would pick a fight with me. I skipped school for days one time when I defended myself from a guy that tried to fight me. I got the best of him too, but was still scared to go to school. My only comfort was to pray to God for courage to go back to school.

Being as poor as we were and some of the unfortunate things that happened to myself and my family during that time, gave you only two ways to think about life:

1) Give up hope and take a bitter and hateful approach to the way one saw life and humanity as a whole, or

2) Keep hope alive and pray to God that this was just part of the plan HE has for you to make you who you were going to become. HE has plans for you.

I took the second option.

Facing my fear.

I was 17 years old and a junior in high school. My mother divorced my father when I was 9 years old and she had remarried a man who lost his job with the B&O railroad and decided to join the military. He was in the U.S. Air Force when he was younger attaining the rank of E-6 (staff sergeant) before leaving the service. He was too old now to be accepted into service by the Air Force, so he tried the U.S. Army. The Army would allow him to enlist at his age (he was 36 at the time), but could not give him his previous rank. He would have to start all over again in basic training as a private (E-1). Left with little opportunity given that he didn't even graduate high school and instead received a general education diploma (G.E.D.), he enlisted in the U.S. Army to provide some kind of income for our family. Accepting 2 teenage kids when you didn't have any of your own proved to be very challenging for all parties involved.

One time when I was 15, I had to stop my stepfather from killing our family dog. Pandy was her name and she was an Afghan breed with a grey coloring and not too long a fur coat as the breed tends to get because she was only about 6 months old. Pandy and our other dog Tia (a tea-cup poodle) were fighting (a rare occurrence) while my mother tried to break them up. When my mother reached down to grab Pandy's collar to pull her away, Pandy turned her head

14

and snapped at my mom. The canine tooth penetrated into my mother's wrist deep enough to create a small hole and bleed profusely. Pandy was still a puppy, but a large one, and she immediately coward in fear after snapping at my mother. Pandy knew she had done wrong and we are a loving family to our animals. We didn't blame her.

Soon after that, my step father came home drunk. He and his fellow soldiers had some drinks after work. He saw what Pandy had done to my mother who was crying from the bite. Pandy was upstairs in my bedroom with the door closed. She really was a sweet dog. My mother told me to protect Pandy or my stepfather would kill her. With my stepfather's upbringing, that is what would happen to any animal that hurt a human. I positioned myself in the middle of the staircase. There were many stairs as this was an apartment in old army housing on the army base. My younger brother by two and half years was downstairs with my mother. My stepfather was a full-grown man at approximately 38 years of age at this time and I was a late blooming pubescent 15-year-old boy. I was already afraid, knowing that I would have to stop in from coming up the stairs. He told me to move out of the way before he even started up the stairs. He reeked of alcohol and I could smell him when he first came in the apartment. Looking up at me as he came around the corner to start his ascension, he had this mean, crazy look on his face as he began to speak. I didn't move. As he came up the stairs, I grew more afraid. I had one hand on the wall to my left and one hand on the banister to my right; forming a barrier with my arms and body. Without laying a hand on me, he came right up to my face. His face was about an inch away from mine. He warned me, "Move out of my way boy!" I stood fast. He said, "That dog has to die!" "Either, that dog dies, or you do!" He then clenched his left fist and raised it up in as a warning and as preparation if I didn't move. I was so scared at this moment. I was already crying and actually thought of moving out of the way because of the fear I felt. However, I knew if I moved, that sweet puppy wouldn't have a chance. I knew I was the only thing stopping her from being killed. I was so scared that I just squinted my eyes and turned my face slightly away from his fist, but held fast my position, fully expecting a beating. Even though I was 15, I was no match for him and I didn't even attempt to fight back. I knew I was going to take a beating, but I know I was going to hold that position as long as I could. I silently prayed to God for the strength.

Scared and crying, his fist flew right by my face and into the wall. It was drywall, so lucky for him there weren't any bricks or wooden studs behind the surface. He pulled his fist out as pieces of drywall came flying out with it. Undeterred, he repositioned his fist up as to strike me. Deathly afraid and crying, I held my position. He could easily get past me by striking me and forcing his way past me, but that would definitely hurt me. I think he knew that he was going to have to hurt me in order to get past. Either not wanting to hurt me out of the kindness of his heart, or weighing the legal ramifications of a domestic assault on his record and the damage it would do his career, he lowered his fist and turned to walk down the stairs and out the front door. My mother, brother, and I were all relieved, but still crying. To spare you the suspense of the outcome, we were able to find Pandy a good home to some acquaintances before my stepfather returned home. It was over.

A Scare My Soul Could Hardly Take

I heard the most annoying sound. It was the sound of my alarm clock going off. I groggily shut it off and sat up in bed turning so my feet would be on the floor. Hunched over with my eyes closed and wanting to go back to sleep, I told myself, "Get up now or you will definitely go back to sleep and be late for the bus.

Presently, I was debating whether to stand up or lay back down to snooze. I forced myself to stand and drag my feet across the floor to turn on my bedroom light on the wall. It was another day of the week. I had to get ready for school. I quickly went into the bathroom to use the facility and threw on some slippers and my robe and took my two dogs (dachshunds) downstairs to go outside to do their business. It was 4:30 am. My mother and stepfather were still asleep in their room, as was my brother who didn't have to get up as early as me on account that he was still in middle school. Middle school for us was 7th, 8th, and 9th grade. We were living on the 4th floor of U.S. housing in a small town called Heubach in West Germany (The Berlin Wall dividing East and West Germany was still in place at this time) in 1985. There was no elevator and the stairs were wide enough for two people at the same time. The stair corridor was immediately out our front door. In the shape of a square, the stairs going both up and down were on the east and west side while the floors in the hallway were on the north and south sides. The dogs and myself had 5 sets of stairs to descend with about 10 stairs for each set. The lights were usually on in the stairway, but not all the lights to save on electricity expenditures. German citizens are highly taxed on everything including power consumption. This was housing leased by the U.S. military for its family personnel some 8 miles away from the U.S. military kasern (small base). The lights were all turned on during high traffic hours.

   This was our daily routine. I got up at 4:30 am to get ready for the day. I had to catch a small german bus in front at my housing building at 6 am that took me and a couple other kids to a larger tour bus at the caserne that left at 6:30 am to travel the hour and a half one way to make it to the school by 8 am. We were always showing up at school as the bell for the first class was sounding.

   The dogs did their business, but being that Germany is high in latitude, it can be cold and the fall through spring months can have a lot of snow on the ground as was the case at this time. The dogs loved to bound in the snow. You couldn't really see them if they stood still, but you could see their whole body when they would jump into the air breaking the top of the snow cover. They did this with such enthusiasm that when I would witness them above the snow drifts with each leap into the air they took, I swear I could detect a gigantic smile across their faces as their tails wagged profusely. It always brought a smile to my face as well. I let them have their fun for a few minutes until I couldn't stand being in the cold any longer or I felt the urgency to hurry as to not be late for the 1st bus.

   I called the dogs in and we trekked up the stairs to our apartment. I threw my robe onto my bed. I was a messy kid and hardly ever cleaned my room. I went directly across the hallway from my bedroom to the family bathroom to take a shower. I was done with my shower, had gotten dressed, and was brushing my teeth in front of the bathroom mirror.

By this time, my stepfather was still sleeping. My mother and brother were both awaked. I could hear both of them in the kitchen just around the corner. I don't know why, but for some reason my mother was washing dishes. We didn't have a dishwasher so my family used to joke to company that we had 2 dishwashers – me and my brother. As one would come out of the hallway into the kitchen, the sink was directly under a window so that if you were facing the sink then your back would be towards the hallway and the living room. I was so puzzled why my mother was doing dishes at this time. I mean, it was so early and she usually had me or my brother do them anyway. All of this seemed strange. Something wasn't right.

As I looked at myself in the mirror while rinsing the toothpaste out of my mouth, I felt this strange feeling overcome me. I turned to look into the hallway where the source of this feeling was coming from. I ended locking my eyes on this small elaborate mirror hanging on the wall in the hallway next to the door of my bedroom. It was my mother's mirror she had bought at an antique store. The mirror itself was only about 7 inches in diameter laid inside an intricate wood frame. The intricate designs in the wood looked like waves of the ocean both above and below the mirror. It looked really old; more than just an antique. To me it looked like it could be ancient. My mother was always shopping at antique stores. Of course, she would only buy antiques that did not have antique pricing. We were on the low-income end of society and my stepfather didn't make a lot of money at a rank of E-4 (specialist). I remember my mother buying this mirror in a store that I thought was creepy to begin with. She got the mirror for almost nothing. She loved it, but it always gave me the creeps. I guess it reminded me of ancient or unknown times. Like many people, I guess I had a fear of the unknown.

As I stared at the mirror in the hallway, I felt hypnotized by it. I was entranced, feeling and almost seeing waves of rings coming from it directed at me. I sensed a feeling of pure evil. This feeling overtook me and made me desire and envision hitting my brother from behind and knocking him to the floor. I then would mount him sitting on his belly in the most dominant position and delighting in biting and tearing the flesh from his face. I could feel his flesh from his face in my hands and how it felt good to squeeze it and try to tear it off of him while he screamed in fear and pain. I was still bigger and stronger than him at this time and there is no way he could defend himself. I delighted in his fear and helplessness. He would surely end up dying from this assault that I envisioned and had the feeling to do. I didn't care and it felt good.

As this feeling enveloped my entire being, I felt that something else was taking over my body. I felt that the real me was still inside my body, but pushed deep down and not in control. I was scared that I could feel the delight at my brother's anguish. I was terrified that it felt so good to hurt him because I truly loved my brother as I did all of my family. As I was still in the bathroom hypnotized by this ancient evil artifact that somehow made it into our home, I started to walk towards it. Still entranced, I lifted it off of the wall and calmly walked around the corner and into the kitchen where my mother was washing dishes. My brother was not in the kitchen. I walked up behind my mother. With the water running from the faucet, my mother did not hear or notice me. I raised the mirror above my head to strike my 4'11" mother on the top of her head with the mirror with the full intention of beating her to death with it. The real me that was pushed deep down in my psyche was fighting hard to gain control to stop what was happening. I was panicked and desperate. I had to gain control. As my arms came down with the mirror, I was able to influence my body to divert my aim from the target of my mother's head just to the side and slammed the mirror on the counter next to the woman who bore me and loved me with all of her heart. Naturally, it startled and frightened her to no end. I was hoping that the mirror would break. It did not, but it did break the spell it had over me.

Ignoring the tongue lashing I was getting from my mother about terrifying her, I was now free from the effects of this evil mirror. I knew now that this mirror was forged by something very evil – an ancient evil lying in wait for an unsuspecting victim. I knew at once I had to destroy it. I raised the mirror above my head again and slammed it down on the hard counter. It did not break. My mother, finger waving and reading me the riot act, was next to me. I quickly opened the window above the sink in the kitchen. My thought was to throw the mirror out of the window on the 4th floor so it would gain enough momentum to shatter upon impact on the concrete below. Being so early in the morning, there was nobody milling about outside. I threw it out and watched as gravity took hold and pulled it toward the ground only to end up landing on a corner of grass directly adjacent to the concrete walkway and parking lot. It didn't break.

I knew I had to destroy this thing. If I didn't, it would claim another innocent victim. I immediately opened the exit door to our apartment and entered the stairway. I noticed the dimly lit platforms and staircase. I felt an evil presence. As I descended the stairway the remaining lights switched off. I could sense the evil in each corner of the stairway where it was darkest and could not be seen. There was enough moonlight to barely see with the lights off in the middle of the stairs. I was terrified because I knew that whatever this evil was, it knew what my intentions were and was determined to stop me. Floor after floor, I felt the presence growing.

As I reached the bottom floor and entrance/exit to the apartment building, I looked into the split-level stairs going down to the basement level where the washing machines were. It was pitch black and I could see nothing. When I opened the glass and aluminum door to go outside, I heard a sound like the gates of hell opening and shutting firmly. I was terrified because I knew something was coming. This evil would not let me reach my goal of destroying this mirror. I ran outside and up the slight grass upgrade to the where the mirror lied. I had just missed the concrete by a few inches. Absolutely terrified I picked the mirror up, making sure not to look into the reflection, and raised it above my head, just as I heard and felt a deep thumping vibration coming from just inside the apartment building. I slammed the mirror down onto the concrete. Astonished and panicking, I realized that it did not break. My heart dropped. Just then as I was picking the mirror up to try again, the door opened. I saw giant red scaly foot with claws touch down on the walkway in front of the door. Subsequently, a hulking humanoid figure started to emerge. This humanoid being was so tall that it had to bend over at the waist almost to 90 degrees in order to clear the 6 and half feet tall doorway. Barely fitting through the width of the door too, up stood a creature I had seen before, but did

not know of its actual existence. Reminding me of the
Devil, was a red scaly efreet. An effreet is a very ancient and
powerful Djinn (Genie). Looking humanoid it had claws on
its feet and hands. Its head was that of a gargoyle with
pointed ears, horns on its head, and large canine teeth that
protruded from the top of its mouth even when it was
closed. It had deep sunken in eyes that glowed a dirty
yellow color. It must have been 12 feet tall or more. I
quickly slammed the mirror on the concrete again to no
avail. (I first read of the Djinn and Efreet in a book of the
role-playing game, 'Dungeons & Dragons'. An efreet is
depicted on the cover of the 'Dungeon Master's Guide'.
That is the creature I was seeing.)

At this moment, my fear overtook me and I abandoned my mission to destroy the artifact to preserve my own life. As the efreet started to take a step in my direction, I turned to run. The creature laughed a deep bellow as I could feel the thump in the vibration of his stepping upon the ground. I could not move. I was frozen and again, not in control of my body. The creature was so large that it would only take 2 more steps for it to be within range to touch me. I was dying inside my own body. I was drowning in indescribable fear and hopelessness. I would be killed and the evil would continue to prey upon the innocent. As the efreet took another step laughing as it did so, I immediately sat up in my bed sweating profusely.

I was still scared to move, but quickly got out of bed and turned the lights on. It was only 3 a.m. and I was scared to be alone. I had never been this way at this age. I was 17 years old and not a mamma's boy. I grabbed my Bible for comfort. I went into the living room and turned on all the lights in the kitchen and living room as well. I was scared to wake my mother and step father as well as embarrassed because I was frightened to be alone. However, I was more scared to be alone and eventually knocked on their bedroom door and woke them up. My mother came out to talk to me. She wanted to go back to bed, but she could tell I was visibly shaken. She stayed with me while I calmed down over the course of an hour. When she finally went back to bed, I only had 30 min. until I had to get up for school, so I spent that time reading my Bible and praying to God for protection. Needless to say, while getting ready for school I did not even glance in the direction of the mirror on the hallway wall which I knew was there. This memory of this nightmare has stayed with me until this day.

First Year of College

There I was in college trying to decide what electives to take during my second semester. I was majoring in biology and minoring in chemistry. Science seemed easy for me to retain over other types of studies and disciplines. My first semester had gone well for me, as I had a 3.6 grade point average taking 32 credit hours in one semester. Starting my second semester now, I had to decide on an elective. There wasn't anything I was really interested in. Why do you have to take electives at all? Why couldn't I just take the "meat and potatoes" of what I needed for my degree? I looked at a home economics course in cooking. I thought, that would come in useful when I was out of the dorms and living totally on my own in my own place. However, I did not enjoy cooking and didn't have much interest in it. In addition, I hated to wash dishes even more than cooking. The unfortunate subsequent activity of cooking, after eating of course, is cleaning up the mess you made in the kitchen. Reluctantly, I started to add that elective to my order form, when I saw something that caught my eye. One of the electives was a class called, "World Religions". Growing up through high school, my faith in God increased dramatically.

While in college, my mother actually was worried about me, because she thought I was getting into 'the Church' too much. She felt I was susceptible to entering a cult. I went to Bible studies and worship gatherings a couple nights during the week as well as on Sundays. The woman that introduced me to Christianity from a very young age and thought it was important to teach me about God, was now worried that I was too much into God. Kind of ironic. I went to worship services more because I was living in the dorms by myself. After graduating high school, I was set on enlisting in the U.S. Army. Knowing we didn't have the money to pay for college and I had no idea of what I wanted to do in life, I thought that joining the military was my only real option.

My mother convinced me to join the Army National Guard as she petitioned the Capt. of the ROTC program at the college to help me fill out grant requests for my schooling if I enrolled in ROTC. I guess I easily qualified for the grant because of our economic status. That is what I did. (A couple years later I ended up dropping ROTC at the end of my sophomore year just before signing my commitment letter to the U.S. Army). I went to Basic Training 4 days after graduating high school and Advanced Individual Training the next summer break. The following semester after Basic Training I was in ROTC at a University in Oklahoma. The grants paid for my classes, dorm, and food in the cafeteria. My spending money outside of that came from being in the Army National Guard (One weekend a month). My mother, brother, and step father had moved far away to another state.

When I started to get more muscular, the bullying slowed down and stopped altogether when I started wrestling my senior year. I was also working out with weights in the gym and started to admire the bodybuilders of the 80's. I worked out 5 to 6 days a week for 3 hours at a time. I was probably overtraining, but I didn't know any better back then. I used to read the magazine, "Muscle and Fitness." The bodybuilding world was still hiding everything that went with it back then, so I thought you could really look like the professional bodybuilders in the magazine if you ate the right foods and worked out properly. Steroids were strongly discouraged in the magazines of the time and the famous bodybuilders would deny they took any kind of drug. Therefore, I too was strongly against taking a steroid for bigger muscle growth. I thought it was cheating. Little did I know that all professional bodybuilders took steroids and growth hormone as well as other drugs. Even the guys in the gym with me that were on the college football team were taking them. I'm sure they thought I was very naive. I was. I eventually succumbed to a couple years of self-inflicted pressure to take anabolic steroids. I got into the bodybuilding scene which I continued throughout college. The girls I used to have a crush on in high school, some of them cheerleaders, all of sudden started to like me. I remember one cute blond girl who was a cheerleader in the high school I graduated from, had the same biology class I did in college. I started to notice her looking at me a lot more. (of course, I wore a lot of tank tops because I liked the attention). She asked me out once knowing that I liked her in high school. I realized, that I didn't like her anymore and I turned her down. My junior I moved to Nebraska to live with my biological father who I had regained communications with just a year before. He invited me to come live with him while I finished up my schooling for my bachelor's degree.

Even my father, who was an atheist and still is today, thought it was stupid that I believed in God. He thought I worked out so much and that I had a great physique. To my father nothing is worth doing unless it is entertaining or it makes you money. My father said to me, "You work out all

the time. Why don't you have it make you some money?"
He suggested that I become a "stripper" (male exotic
dancer) part time while I go to school. I was still a shy kid,
but coming out of my shell so to speak. My father took me
by the hand to couple places in town to see if they would
hire me. I think my father was actually living vicariously
through me. He always flaunted himself as a "ladies' man".
I was shy and it took quite a while to the point of no return.
One night, the owner of the establishment, said "you need
to make a decision tonight whether you want to do this or
not. Given the ultimatum, I forced myself through the fear
and received a very approving, thunderous ovation from the
host crowd of women. The rest is now history. I worked as
an exotic dancer full-time for 5 years even after graduating
with my bachelor's degree in Biology and minoring in
Chemistry. I had a conundrum all throughout this
profession. I still had a strong belief in God and what I was
taught to be right and wrong, but somehow justified what I
was doing to make money because it was easy and it gave
me the attention that fully brought me out of my shell.

However, with this lifestyle it is very difficult to avoid
certain types of people and activities. One of which is drugs
and drug dealers. I remember one night I accompanied a
female friend to a so-called party. She was just my friend
and I had dated a couple of her friends and she had dated
two guys (not at the same time) that I introduced her to
that were very significant to her life. She was an attractive
girl and did not want to go to this party alone. So, I went
with her. The party, it so happens, turned out to be 2 guys
that had a hotel room at one of the local casino's and my
friend and I. I sensed the 2 guys were not pleased with
seeing me with her. Having the physique that I did, they

were obviously intimidated and neither said anything threatening to me. But I still didn't think I was safe around them. Regardless of my physique, it was two of them against just one of me.

They brought out a bunch of cocaine, which I adamantly refused at first, but was persuaded to take part by all parties that were present. We ended up doing this all night and it became apparent to me that these 2 strange men that I just met were dealers and were growing more and more upset that I was there accompanying my female friend. I had a high tolerance and did a line every 20 minutes for hours on end. When I sensed that this situation could turn violent, I told my female friend that we needed to leave. The 2 men were not happy. I was in no condition to drive. I ended up getting my friend back to her parent's house (yes, in her 20's and still at home). I then tried to make it home to my apartment. (I lived alone). It was winter time and it was Nebraska, so there was already a ton of snow on the ground, it was about 5:30 am, it was still dark outside and a blizzard was rolling in. I was fighting to stay awake. Usually cocaine is a stimulant, but if you've been doing it all night, your body is exhausted and it just wants to shut down. I was praying to God to be with me and to get me home safe. I was so remorseful. Angry at myself for even taking part in a felony drug. How could I have been so stupid? Concentrating on the street signs that I could barely focus on and trying not to wreck my car in the snow and heavier and heavier snowflakes that were coming down, I continued to pray out loud. I was talking to God like he was right there by my side in the passenger seat. I was scared, because I didn't want to get hurt or crash my car and freeze to death which has happened on a couple of occasions to people where I am from. I, too, did not want to get stopped by the police. It was obvious to anyone that I was impaired.

I don't know how long had passed until I wondered why I wasn't home yet. I finally saw a sign on the Interstate and realized I was half way to Kansas City. I had taken a left when I should have gone right when the interstate forked. My throat dropped to the pit of my stomach. It took everything I had to stay awake to this point. I was in desperation. I prayed harder to just let me get home safe. I made a U-turn. I did everything I could to keep my body from shutting down. I turned up the radio really loud. I periodically would roll down the windows to get a blast of frigid air to my face until I couldn't stand the cold. I continued to pray to God until finally, I did make it home safe. I slept for almost 16 hours. When I awoke, I thanked God for getting me through it. I felt there was no way I could have survived that without some kind of divine help. I never did cocaine again.

However, this took place after college. I digress.

Back to this elective of "World Religions". I was reluctant to enroll because I was always taught by the church to never read anything other than the Bible. However, I was curious to know why other people believed the way they did. If anything, it would help me relate to others when talking to them and trying to spread the Gospel. I checked the box and enrolled.

A Survey of the World's Major Religions

Chapter 3

A Different Perspective

The class World Religions was a lot more interesting to me than I had thought. After all, every religion in the world teaches that it is the only true religion and that all others are wrong. Christianity was no different. Even though I was learning about other World Religions, I still felt Christianity was the true religion. Why wouldn't I? I had known nothing else growing up. All of the ancient civilization's religions were pagan religions, or worshiped a pantheon of Gods. Hinduism which is a popular religion in the world today mainly in India is still a pantheon of Gods that are worshiped. The Abrahamic Faiths (Judaism, Christianity, and Islam) are in contrast to that and are monotheistic, or worshiping one "true" God. These three faiths can be broken down into sub-categories which we won't bother going into here. These three faiths are the most dominant on the planet. I guess you could add another faith that dominates a large amount of the population, or lack of faith, and that would be Atheism (the belief that there are no Gods). The far eastern religions of the Orient, such as Buddhism and Taoism do not have Gods so to speak, but revere great human teachers that brought the knowledge of each person's spirit to the masses.

The one thing inherent in all the religions of the world (except atheism) is belief in an afterlife. The hope that life continues after physical death of your body. Why is this? Is there something to this? Perhaps some lost ancient texts that all the religions drew this conclusion from? Or, perhaps it is what every person hopes for in order to keep us focused on our daily tasks so we don't spend our lives worrying that one day life will be over and we will cease to exist? As of yet modern science has not been able to prove one way or the other about the ending or continuation of life after physical death. Perhaps our technology is not yet sophisticated enough to detect matters of the spirit? It is this author's belief that the spirit or soul is a natural occurrence to a living physical body that is perfectly in sync with the universe and the laws of physics. We, as a society, just have not reached that level of technological sophistication in order to detect that type of energy.

Perhaps one day, we will develop such technology and put the question to rest? Where would this spirit go? Heaven? Nirvana? Brahman-Atman? All of these concepts tend to be in the direction of "up", as in, "our spirit will go up to Heaven." What is it we see when we look "up?" While I sat in the first class the professor started to go over the general introduction to the class and I started to think. (Daydream)

Have you ever looked up at the night sky, at the multitude of stars and planets, space related phenomena and thought, If God made the Earth and humans and every living thing, why wouldn't He create other life elsewhere in this vast Universe, of which Earth is just a speck of dust compared to the eternal expansion of space? I'm sure most of us have. At this point in time, modern science has discovered the structure of our solar system, many exoplanets outside of our solar system, and many stars, galaxies, and phenomena that take place far, far away from us in space.

For those of you who aren't familiar with our local astronomy, our solar system begins with the center of it: The Sun. The next closest planet to the Sun would be the tiny planet of Mercury. Venus would follow Mercury in proximity to the Sun followed by Earth and then Mars. These 4 planets are called the "inner planets" because they lie between the Sun and a ring of rocky asteroids that are abundant around the entire orbit that circumference the Sun. Outside of the Asteroid Belt that it's been named are the much larger "outer planets". Leaving the Asteroid Belt, we would first encounter the giant planet of Jupiter. Next would be Saturn which is distinguishable by its many rings. Next would be Uranus followed by Neptune. The last object that we once considered a planet was the small object named Pluto. Pluto was demoted from a planet to a planetoid or dwarf planet in 2006 by the International Astronomical Union (IAU).

To summarize, we have the Sun/ (inner planets) Mercury, Venus, Earth, Mars/ Asteroid Belt/ (outer planets) Jupiter, Saturn, Uranus, Neptune. 4 inner planets and 4 outer planets separated by the Asteroid Belt. Each planet has varying amounts of moons, but in total there are 92 heavenly bodies surrounding the Sun (not including asteroids, comets, and debris).

This knowledge of the structure of our solar system will be relevant in a later chapter of this book. An interesting point is that all of these planets and the asteroid belt lie in the same plane or angle to the Sun. Think of a paper plate and you put marbles on the plate to represent the planets without rolling around. They would be the same level and at the same angle relative to the center of the plate. All of our planets are this way relative to our Sun. This plane that they lie in is called the 'ecliptic'.

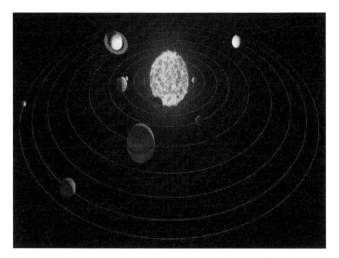

All of a sudden, I was startled. I was poked by my classmate beside me who obviously noticed I was daydreaming. At the same time, it was accompanied by the sound of books slamming shut. It was time for class to be over. I gathered up my things and headed back to the dorms. To save you from the boring story that was my college life, I will fast forward. I graduated with a Bachelor of Science degree in Biology with a minor in Chemistry, just shy of a couple classes to qualify me for a degree in Biotechnology. God was always a part of my life and I prayed frequently (not as much as I was taught to) to Him for help with my schoolwork, or family matters, financial matters, and my love-life (I didn't have one but prayed to have one.) I was a shy kid and didn't end up kissing a girl for the first time until I was 21 years of age. (Yes, it's true.)

Starting early on in my life, I have always been inquisitive. I wanted to know or discover what other people hadn't. Especially if I could never get a definitive answer. Space has always fascinated me. Just like foreign countries used to. I have traveled overseas, and now with the internet, it doesn't seem so alluring like it was before. However, space and other planets are still interesting to me. I guess because even our most brilliant astronomers and astronauts are still just beginning to learn more about space. Mankind has been to the Moon and back, but only a handful of humans have ever really been there and none have spent much time on the surface. So really, we don't know that much about our own Moon, let alone other heavenly bodies. We have launched probes that have sent some pictures and data in passing the planets back to Earth, but this is far from really knowing that much. It is like we are starving and we get our first scraps from a decked out, long table adorned with different types of food and delicacies. We are so hungry for more.

If God created life here on Earth, doesn't it make sense that He would create it on other planets as well? However, the Bible doesn't say this. The church teaches that we humans are the pinnacle of God's creation. He has given us 'free-will', which we are taught, not even the angels have. We are taught that this makes us special over the angels. We are taught that God is an entirely different being than the angels which He created before mankind. For centuries you would have been burned at the stake for even mentioning that there could be life out in the universe or that the Earth was not the center of it, just like Giordano Bruno on February 17th, 1600 a.d. in Rome for believing in exoplanets.

Some of my favorite TV shows were, Star Trek, BattleStar Galactica, Lost in Space, Buck Rogers in the 24th century, Space 1999 (funny what the writers envisioned we would have as far as technology. 1999 came and went and we quit going to the moon after the Apollo missions.) Some movies that I liked were Invasion of the Body Snatchers, Close Encounters of the 3rd Kind, Star Wars, the Alien series, Star-man, the Star Trek movies, E.T., The Abyss, ect.

These were popular shows, so I guess I wasn't the only one who liked these shows not only about the possibility of life in space, but the possibility of intelligent life that was equal to or greater technologically than own Earth civilizations. I always wondered about space and intelligent life beyond our own world. In the early 2000's, I worked in Executive Protection to a firm that held some of the world's wealthiest billionaires as clients. Some of the same people you here about in world news with fortune 500 companies, as well as, Hollywood actors and actresses. I am still under a 50-year confidentiality clause so I can't go into a who's who list of names.

In executive protection there is a lot of time spent monitoring surveillance cameras for very long hours. Often, especially if you happened to get the night shift, there isn't really too much going on. To stay alert and to stop from falling asleep, the firm I worked for actually encouraged its employees keep their minds active by reading or looking at the internet, ect. Anything really to stop you from breaking the #1 rule: Don't fall asleep. If you did, the disciplinary action would be instant termination of employment. We were all on camera anyway, so you would have to be pretty dumb to allow yourself to fall asleep when some supervisor could tell you were sleeping from anywhere in the world by accessing the internet and connecting to your respective camera feed. However, there were still some people that allowed themselves to get too comfortable and lost their job in the process. Needless to say, I was not one of those individuals. Actually, I was one of the firms new "golden boys." Whatever they asked of me, I said yes. This allowed me to be assigned to some details overseas and to other States in the U.S. that many other agents would have to work some years and "pay their dues" before being picked to do these types of details that I was immediately getting. It was a good experience for me. Being around the rich and famous up close taught me that the hype around such figures is imaginary and downright stupid.   I came to realize that they are people, just like any other person, but with money and/or fame.

It didn't change my life any. While I am looking at the client's brand-new Bentley automobile on their property I, however, still go home to my 1-bedroom apartment in my basic compact sedan.   The illusion that protecting the rich and famous made my unimportant life somehow more alluring, wore off on me quite rapidly.   When my wife was pregnant with our 2nd child, I had to quit saying "yes" to the company. No more traveling around the world for weeks at a time leaving my wife to work full-time and take care of an infant with another on the way.   Needless to say, I lost my "golden boy" status and fell out of favor with management. Doing nothing wrong of course, I just continued to work at my designated post at my primary principle's residence (rich/famous client's home). Myself, still being somewhat of a new hire, I drew the night shift most of the time. This, in turn, allowed me to research topics I might be interested in. One of these topics was UFO's.

It is absolutely fascinating to me that when you look at the history of UFO's (Unidentified Flying Objects) in the United States, that 95% of the population has no frame of reference to what is actually documented and what is purely fiction. Most people think that there is nothing documented and any UFO incident that was ever documented was explainable by natural causes or misidentified objects.

During my research then until now, I have come upon many cases that are likely true, but have been classified by the government and I, not having the clearance, have had to rely on leaks about the incidents. Because these encounters are classified, there is no way that you or I can truly know if they happened or not. At least until they declassify them. "Don't hold your breath." For these reasons I won't go into those cases, but I will go over some of the documented cases that anyone has access to if they just put a little effort looking into it.

Aurora, Texas Incident

Before the modern era of UFO's and before mankind had discovered the technology of flight, there was an incident in Aurora, Texas on Saturday April 17th, 1897 at 6am. A resident witness was S.E. Hayden and he told the Dallas Morning News of its time, this UFO was built of "an unknown m: A cigar-shaped UFO, metallic silver in color, appeared suddenly in the sky above Aurora. It was moving from south to north. Unlike the balloon airships etal, resembling somewhat a mix of aluminum and silver." A witness guessed that the ship weighed "several tons."

The strange craft seemed to be having some kind of mechanical problems. It slowed down to about ten or twelve miles per hour and began settling toward the ground.

Haydon said the townspeople watched in amazement as the slow-moving airship drifted over the town square and then moved north toward the property of Judge J. S. Proctor. Next, the UFO collided with a windmill on the judge's land and "went into pieces with a terrific explosion, scattering debris over several acres of ground." The crash destroyed the windmill, the adjacent water tank and the judge's flower garden.

Among the debris, was the body of the pilot. Although burned and deceased, it was clear to witnesses that the pilot was not human. This was said by T.J. Weems who inspected the crash site and was an officer in the U.S. Cavalry Signal Corps. T.J. Weems was also an amateur astronomer. Weems told the Dallas Morning News that the pilot, "was not an inhabitant of this world" and "may have been from Mars." Much of the debris was hauled off by townspeople and a large bulk of it was thrown down the well on the Judges property. That well was later capped from a later owner who bought the property. That well remains sealed today and attempts by people to petition the owner to open it to conduct testing on any materials at the bottom have failed. The body of the pilot was given a proper Christian burial in the town cemetery. This story did not become popular until the 1970's. Jim Mars, a UFO researcher, visited the cemetery and saw the grave of the pilot was marked by small headstone. When he went to receive permission to excavate the grave, he discovered that the headstone had been removed and the grave as well. Later technology was used, such as ground penetrating radar, to try and locate the pilot's body with negative results. Do not be so quick to disregard these witnesses as being inept because they lived in 1897 as opposed to today. They may not have had our newer technology, but they were just as intelligent as we are now. Some would argue more so.

A Windmill Demolishes It.

Aurora, Wise Co., Tex., April 17.—(To The News.)—About 6 o'clock this morning the early risers of Aurora were astonished at the sudden appearance of the airship which has been sailing through the country.

It was traveling due north, and much nearer the earth than ever before. Evidently some of the machinery was out of order, for it was making a speed of only ten or twelve miles an hour and gradually settling toward the earth. It sailed directly over the public square, and when it reached the north part of town collided with the tower of Judge Proctor's windmill and went to pieces with a terrific explosion, scattering debris over several acres of ground, wrecking the windmill and water tank and destroying the judge's flower garden.

The pilot of the ship is supposed to have been the only one on board, and while his remains are badly disfigured, enough of the original has been picked up to show that he was not an inhabitant of this world.

Mr. T. J. Weems, the United States signal service officer at this place and an authority on astronomy, gives it as his opinion that he was a native of the planet Mars.

Papers found on his person—evidently the record of his travels—are written in some unknown hieroglyphics, and can not be deciphered.

The ship was too badly wrecked to form any conclusion as to its construction or motive power. It was built of an unknown metal, resembling somewhat a mixture of aluminum and silver, and it must have weighed several tons.

The town is full of people to-day who are viewing the wreck and gathering specimens of the strange metal from the debris. The pilot's funeral will take place at noon to-morrow. S. E. HAYDON.

Actual Newspaper Article from Dallas Morning News, 4-19-1897

Although, the case above and many other incidents go back throughout history, the modern era of UFO's started in 1947. The demarcation timeline starts with Kenneth Arnold, a private pilot and member of the Idaho Search and Rescue Mercy Flyers, who on June 24th 1947, joined a search mission to locate a missing Marine transport plane that was believed to have crashed in the Cascade Mountains of Washington State. While flying at an altitude of 9,000 feet, Arnold saw 9 silvery craft flying in formation directly across his flight path. Each craft looked like a crescent moon, but a little thicker in the middle with a tail or point coming from the middle of the crescent. Using landmarks, he knew with the backdrop of Mount Raniere, Arnold timed the formation between the landmarks and was able to calculate their speed being 1700 miles per hour. A full 1000 miles per hour faster than the current world air speed record of that time. Arnold was not the only witness to these craft. Pilots flying a nearby DC-4 also saw the craft, as well as, hundreds of people on the ground. Arnold gave an interview to the East Oregonian newspaper and said, "they flew as if a saucer would if you skipped it across water."

When the Associated Press picked up the story, they took Arnold's statement and coined the term "Flying Saucers" which then became an integral part of our language.

Below is a picture of Arnold with a depiction of what he said each craft looked like.

with Friedman. Along with bringing the Roswell Crash to the public, Friedman also brought to light the first government agency who was commissioned to deal with all UFO related material – MJ-12 in his book "MJ-12 (Top secret/Majic)." Then came probably the most famous case in Ufology:

The Roswell Incident (Crash)

On July 4th, 1947, late at night there was a thunderstorm and a supposed UFO disappeared off of the radar of CIC Army radar observer Sgt. Frank Kaufman and crashed in the desert near Roswell, New Mexico. The UFO contained 4 alien bodies, one of which actually survived the crash. According to Col. Philip Corso, who was the assistant to Lt. General Trudeau at the Army's Research and Development department at the Pentagon between 1961 – 1963, two of those aliens would have survived, but being shortly after WWII the soldiers that responded to the crash and set up a perimeter were a little quick on the trigger. The bodies laid about close to the craft, but when surveying the area, one of the aliens got up and tried to scurry over a sand dune. Before the ranking officer on site could say "hold your fire", many servicemen had already shot the creature. I say creature, because the bodies did not look human. They would be described what has come to be known as a typical "Grey". The movie "Close Encounters of the Third Kind" came really close to portraying what they looked like 4 to 4.5 ft tall. Humanoid in appearance with think torsos and their 2 arms and 2 legs were slender. They had a very large head with a skinny neck. Large, black wrap around almond shaped eyes with no nose and just a slit for a mouth. All of this was covered in Colonel Corso's book, "The Day After Roswell" (co-authored by William J. Birnes) in which he explains that he personally received 5 artifacts from the UFO crash site with a file at the Pentagon from Lt. General Trudeau. He was instructed to personally deliver these artifacts to American business military contractors to reverse engineer them to add to our own projects that were currently ongoing. Col. Corso said he did this and the reason we are much more advanced in the areas of Fiberoptics, Lasers, Nightvision, Integrated Circuitry and Body Armor, are from advances made by the reverse engineering of these artifacts. Another artifact in Col. Corso's possession was a proposed navigational instrument that was placed on the pilot's head. Reportedly, they never could get it to work. Colonel Corso stated in his book that those artifacts is all he received from the crash. He stated that the craft itself, which was mostly intact, was hauled off and in possession of the Army Air Corps. (a prelude department to the not yet existing military branch, the U.S. Air Force)

The 2 days before the Roswell Incident, 3 different radar systems from 3 different Military bases in the area tracked UFO's on radar, accompanied by hundreds of civilian witnesses reporting seeing UFO's in the sky.

Mac Brazel was manager of the Foster Ranch. He discovered some of the UFO debris on his client's land. He was the first to contact authorities.

(Sidebar – this is the same Mac Brazel that was 10 years old when his family ambushed and murdered the famous lawman Pat Garrett who himself was famous for shooting and killing William Bonney or "Billy the Kid." Mac might have even taken part in the ambush.)

After the night of tremendous thunderstorms, Mac Brazel decided to check on the livestock. So, riding a horse and accompanied by 7 years old William D. Proctor, he came upon the debris of the crash in a pasture. The debris resembled smooth tinfoil and light "I" beams with strange hieroglyphic symbol writing. Years later, both William Brazel Jr (Mac Brazel's son) and Jesse Marcel Jr. (Son of the Major Jesse Marcel who was the intelligence officer of the 509th bomber group at Roswell, New Mexico and accompanied Mac Brazel back to the debris field) said when interviewed that the smooth tinfoil metal could not be scratched wrinkled or burned. Very lightweight, it would unravel itself if crumbled up to become its original and smooth shape. Initially, the Intelligence officer, Jesse Marcel was told to tell the local radio station that the U.S. Army had retrieved a flying saucer which was then broadcast to the public airwaves. The next day, the Army informed the radio station that the craft that crashed was not a flying saucer, but a simple weather balloon, which became the "official" story.

This was the Roswell Incident in a nutshell. So many other stories are intertwined with this one. Some stories say there were actually 2 UFO's that crashed in different areas. Some say 3 actually crashed, two being retrieved by the government subsequently to their crash and the other not being discovered until 1949. Whatever the case may be, the public tended to strictly believe the government story back in 1947. The story faded quickly and really didn't surface again until Stanton Friedman, a nuclear physicist, author, lecturer and UFO researcher brought it to light in 1978. Friedman took a scientific approach to his research. He discovered the "official" government coverup by interviewing Major Jesse Marcel who quit speaking about the event after it happened (as all good officers would do). Retired and out of the military, he was candid

EXTRATERRESTRIAL
ENTITIES AND TECHNOLOGY,
RECOVERY AND DISPOSAL

TOP SECRET/MAJIC
EYES ONLY

WARNING! This is a TOP SECRET—MAJIC EYES
ONLY document containing compartmentalized
information essential to the national security of the
United States. EYES ONLY ACCESS to the material
herein is strictly limited to personnel possessing
MAJIC—12 CLEARANCE LEVEL. Examination or
use by unauthorized personnel is strictly forbidden
and is punishable by federal law.

MAJESTIC—12 GROUP • APRIL 1954

This began the UFO modern era. This is all well and good, but critics of Earth being visited by intelligent alien life always say, "Why don't the UFO's land on the White House lawn?" Then they would probably believe it. On the nights of July 19th and 20th, 1952 almost the equivalent of landing at the White House lawn happened. On those nights 8 flying disks were observed flying over the White House, the Capitol Building, and the Pentagon. The objects were followed by witnesses on the ground, tracked on radar by control towers at D.C.'s National Airport and Andrews Airforce Base, and visually observed by the pilots that were scrambled to intercept the objects to deter them away from restricted air space. The disks moved slowly and at times accelerated to impossible velocities as they flew over the Capitol Building. The jet aircraft that were scrambled to intercept could not keep up. The disks could simply outrun, out maneuver, and outfly anything that the military defense command had existing at that time of our technological flight capabilities. Perhaps even then, the disks would be far more advance then anything we have today.

The disks suddenly vanished from radar only to appear miles away almost instantaneously. This happened on two consecutive nights with the jets scrambled having the same helpless result. The airspace intrusions seemed to stop until a week later, when the disks appeared again over the same airspace on July 26th and again the next night on July 27th. The objects were able to continually penetrate restricted airspace at will. Needless to say, you can imagine how scared our military leaders were for our National Security. This story made headlines with all of the local newspapers, "UFO's Over Capitol". USAF Major General John Samford called a press conference in an effort to calm the public over the UFO invasion. The military's explanation seemed to suffice for most of the population. The sightings were "illusions" caused by temperature inversions that caused "ghost" images in the air as well as on radar. The pilots who chased the disks and visually saw them, later told UFO investigators that they were real, but they were ordered by their superiors to forget what they saw and deny they had ever made contact with such objects. To this day there has never been an official adequate explanation of what actually happened on those dates over Washington D.C. in 1952. Most of the population on Earth today has no idea that this actually took place and is documented and not some made up story.

That same year of 1952, the government started "Project Blue Book" that was run by the U.S. Air Force. "Project Blue Book" was a public reporting attempt by the Air Force to gather information from people calling in on any UFO related sightings. Unknown to the public, in 1949 the C.I.A. funded "Project Sign" that gathered the same type of information, but secretly. Then "Project Sign" was leaked to the press but did not garner any attention. As a result of the leak, the C.I.A. changed the name of the project to "Project Grudge." "Project Grudge" became "Project Blue Book" when the project went public and switched hands to the Air Force. The lead evaluator of reports for "Project Blue Book" was Dr. J. Allen Hynek. Dr. Hynek was well respected by academics and he was the Chairman of the Astronomy Department and Chicago's Northwestern University. He actually started with "Project Sign" and continued through "Project Grudge" and into "Project Blue Book". He was a skeptic to begin with and because of his experience with evaluating all of the reports over the years, he became a believer. He became disillusioned by the Air Force stonewalling at acknowledging that many of the reports had merit by the overwhelming preponderance of the affirmative evidence. When "Project Blue Book" was shut down in 1969, most likely because of the Condon Report, Dr. Hynek became one of the founders of the Center for UFO Studies (CUFOS). Before Dr. Hynek died in 1986 he said, "When the long-awaited solution to the UFO problem comes, I believe that it will prove to be not merely the next small step in the march of science but a mighty and totally unexpected quantum jump." It was Dr. Hynek that came up with the different classifications of UFO encounters.

Radar Visuals

Where UFO's can be tracked on radar and can be visually seen at the same place illustrated at the same time. A good example is a UFO seen visually and on radar pacing behind a commercial jet and then suddenly travels to 7,000 miles per hour in the opposite direction or straight up. Even today it is hard to believe that mankind could create a classified project craft that can maneuver like that. Definitely not 20 to 60 years ago.

1. Close Encounters of the First Kind

   A UFO in close proximity (within approximately 500 feet) to the witness.

2. Close Encounters of the Second Kind

A UFO that leaves markings on the ground, causes burns or paralysis to humans, frightens animals, or interferes with automobile engines or television and radio reception.

3. Close Encounters of the Third Kind

A UFO which has viable occupants.

* Two other classifications later added to Hynek's original list are:

4. Close Encounters of the Fourth Kind

These include alien abduction cases.

5. Close Encounters of the Fifth Kind

Where communication occurs between a human and an alien being.

In 1969 the government decided to call for a committee to settle the question of UFO's once and for all. An independent investigation into the existence of UFO's was conducted by a University of Colorado panel Chaired by Dr. Edward U. Condon. Condon was a nuclear physicist who had worked on the Manhattan Project during World War II. The U.S. Air Force determined that UFO's did not exist and therefore did not pose a threat to the United States National Security, but they needed somebody to "rubber stamp" it so the government could get out of the "flying saucer business". When asked about the matter of UFO's before even beginning to study the evidence, Condon himself said," I'm not supposed to say anything until the panel had come to a conclusion, but it is my opinion that there is nothing to it." Showing bias from the start, this was anything but an unbiased independent investigation. The panel (really just Condon himself) came to the conclusion that UFO's did not exist; however, Condon's conclusions were completely at variance with the rest of the 36 members panel on the University of Colorado Study, which determined that UFO's were a real phenomenon which needed further study. Because Condon was somewhat famous in his circles, his opinion seemed to overshadow the others. This led to the U.S. Air Force officially shutting down "Project Blue Book." Many people think the government did listen to other members on the panel and continued to investigate UFO reports, but not publicly. Some other government agency took over the investigations such as the CIA, NSA, DIA, ect. Since the Condon report showed that UFO's do not exist, the official government stance has been to ridicule or characteristically destroy any witnesses to such events. That exact same stance has been used right up until today. Since much of the population only believes what the government tells them, it would be hard to get somebody to believe you if you told them that you witnessed a UFO, that is, unless they have researched the subject and found there is much more to it than public opinion.

A large percentage of the general public was more open to the idea of UFO's and aliens during the 50's and 60's then they are today, that is, until the government issued its response to the phenomena. Everything changed after the Condon Report. Even the first Director of the C.I.A., (1947-1950) Admiral Roscoe Hillenkoetter believed that UFO's were real. Supposedly one of the members of MJ-12, after retiring, Admiral Hillenkoetter joined the group National Investigations Committee on Aerial Phenomena or (NICAP). Hillenkoetter wrote:

{It's time for the truth to be brought out in open congressional hearings. Behind the scenes, high ranking Air Force officers are soberly concerned about

UFO's. Bet through official secrecy and ridicule, many citizens are led to believe the unknown flying objects are nonsense. To hide the facts, the Air Force has silenced its personnel though the issuance of a regulation.}

Unfortunately, not all of the people in government felt the same way he did.

The case of Betty and Barney Hill

Another important UFO case in history is the case of Betty and Barney Hill. This case was important on many levels and it was the first case of a Close Encounter of the Fourth Kind in the modern era. On September 19th, 1961 the New England couple of Betty and Barney Hill were driving home at night along a country road in rural New Hampshire when they realized they were being tracked by a bright light in the sky. Barney eventually stopped the car when the bright light appeared on the road in front of them. The next thing they knew they were back on the road heading for home, but it was two hours later and they couldn't account for the missing time.

Months late, after Barney's continued bouts of anxiety and physical symptoms, the couple sought medical attention. Their doctor couldn't find any underlying medical problems and recommended they visit a psychiatrist, Dr. Benjamin Simon. Dr. Simon used hypnotic-regression on both Betty and Barney separately and recorded their stories of an abduction by strange beings who took them aboard a spaceship.

- (**<u>Side Note:</u>** *An interesting fact is that Betty and Barney Hill were an inter-racial couple. We all know that some people like to get attention by concocting unbelievable stories of aliens and spaceships, just to get attention. However, giving the social climate of the early 60's and the many tensions raised between race relations at the time, why would Betty and Barney Hill want to have any attention at all unless their story was true. You would think an inter-racial couple would avoid attention to their marriage, let alone the kind of attention their story would bring. Actually, the couple did not want the publicity that came with them seeking medical help.*)

Betty Hill believes that Dr. Simon's assistant, who had access to the notes the psychiatrist made, delivered the Hills' case file to a writer for the *Boston Globe*, who printed the story in the newspaper. That was how their abduction became known to the public.

One of the more remarkable aspects of the Hill case is the Betty was able to sketch a "star map" while under hypnosis, reproducing in detail the map her alien abductors had shown her aboard their spacecraft. She was told that the map showed nearby inhabited planets. At the time, astronomers were not able to recognize what she had drawn. However, as time went on and technology got better, astronomers were amazed to see that her sketch matched the Zeta Reticulli system perfectly when seen from Earth. Betty's sketch was detailed and pinpointed her abductors home world which orbited within that twin star system. Another interesting note is that Betty described one of the medical procedures her abductors did to her on the ship. It involved inserting a very long needle into her naval which Betty recalled as being very painful. She asked her abductors why they were doing this procedure. She recalled that they said it was a test for pregnancy. Remember, this was in 1961. Amniocentesis was not commonly used in medical facilities until 1965. It is a test for pregnancy and many genetic disorders that can arise during the pregnancy.

Barney Hill died in 1969. After his death, Betty was approached by actor James Earl Jones, who was fascinated with the story of the abduction. Jones produced a movie for television in which he played Barney Hill and the role of Betty Hill was played by Estelle Parsons. It was one of the first documentary-dramas about a supposed real UFO encounter. Betty Hill died on Oct. 17th, 2004 at the age of 85 having never remarried.

Betty and Barney Hill

The Travis Walton Case

When Travis Walton was 22 years old, he was working on a federal logging contract in the Apache-Sitgreaves National Forest in Snowflake, Arizona. While driving home one evening after a long day of work, Travis and his 5 co-workers in a truck with him observed a hovering disc like craft just off of the main road. The disc drew them closer. All were a little frightened knowing what they were witnessing from the safety of their vehicle. Travis, being young and wanting to impress his co-workers, decided to get out of the vehicle and according to him, "show off" by acting like he wasn't afraid and walking closer to the craft. Disregarding the yelling of his co-workers to get back inside the vehicle, A beam of white light instantly emitted out of the hovering craft and hit Travis, bathing him in a white light and paralyzing him. The beam seemed to lift Travis off of his feet and knock him backwards some 20 feet or more. Travis did not move and does not recall being knocked unconscious. His co-workers, thinking he was dead, were scared. They panicked and drove off without him speeding away from the disc. Miles down the road, the workers debated among themselves to return and save Travis, feeling guilty that they abandoned him. Finally, they got their courage up and turned the truck around. When they got back to the location, the disc was gone and so was Travis.

The loggers went into town immediately to tell the local sheriff what had happened. Some of the crew urged the others not to tell the truth, because nobody would believe them. The consensus was to tell the truth. As expected, nobody believed them. The Sheriff, Sank Flake, doubted their story and thought they had killed Travis and concocted this amazing story. A massive search party was organized and the search for Travis Walton (or his body) lasted 5 whole days. During this time, Sheriff Flake suggested they all take a polygraph test. All passed the polygraph except one which was "inconclusive." The one man that did not pass had a history of being arrested by law enforcement. That same man in later years passed many polygraphs about this case. Sheriff Flake still did not believe them and had indictments for murder brought up on all the crew members. The indictments had not yet been handed down when Travis Walton was discovered dazed and confused walking on the highway in nearby Heber, Arizona.

Sheriff Flake still did not believe their story. He thought that the crew had made up the story and Travis' disappearance for a publicity stunt to get attention, despite Travis passing his polygraph test. To this day, not one person on that crew has recanted their story and Travis Walton has passed no less than 19 polygraph tests administered by law enforcement examiners. The only polygraph that Travis Walton did not pass is the one where he agreed to be on a gameshow called "The Moment of Truth" on FOX network. When asked if he'd been abducted by aliens, Travis responded with an emphatic, "Yes!" The detector determined he was lying, but the show, the test, and the examiner were dubious. The show was meant to ridicule and discredit guests by supposedly catching them in lies that would be shocking to the guest's families as well as the audience. This case is famous in the annals of UFO history, so much so that a movie was made about this case called "Fire in the Sky" 1993.

(Side note: The movie "Fire in the Sky" in my opinion, was interesting as well as entertaining whether you're a "believer" or not. The abduction was the backstory to the main focus, which was the crew dealing with all the disbelief and ridicule they received from people they had known all their lives and how the townsfolk turned on them and their families.)

Travis Walton supposedly suffering from what is now known as PTSD underwent hypnotic regression for therapy and now has remembered more details about his event.

Travis woke up groggy and confused on what seemed to be a medical table. He noticed 3 small creatures in orange suits coming towards him in a small room. The creatures could now be described as Greys. 3 ½ - 5 ½ feet tall with bald, bulbous heads and spindly bodies with large eyes. Travis was frightened and backed up off of the table to the wall of the room. He felt an object on a shelf behind him which he immediately grabbed to use as a weapon. The creatures continued toward him until they saw him raise his hand with the object in it prepared to strike. That is when the creatures suddenly stopped all at once. In unison, they turned around and exited what seemed to be the only door to the room. Travis slowly made his way to the doorway, looked outside and realized the creatures were gone and there was a hallway. He dropped the object in his hand and tried to find a way out of his environment, coming to a doorway of another room. He went inside the room where there was nothing on the walls because it looked like a clear glass dome looking into space. He could see stars as tiny specs of light. In the center of the room was a chair. He examined the chair and there was what seemed to be a ball not unlike a ball inside a mouse to move a cursor on a computer. Travis touched and moved the ball which immediately made him feel disoriented and dizzy because when he moved the ball, the entire room seemed to move or the dome itself. The stars and whole sky of space moved. Travis later considered this a map or navigation room. However fascinated as he was, he once again realized his urgency to escape. He turned toward the doorway only to see a man there. The man was Caucasian, tall (est. 6 ½ feet), muscular, wearing a form fitting blue jumpsuit. The man had very light blond hair and very light blue eyes. The length was mid length to about the collar. Ecstatic and overjoyed to see another human, Travis went up to him and kept babbling if he knew the way out and they had to get out of there. The "Man" did not say a word, but smiled, and put his arm around the neck and shoulders of Travis and lead him down the hallway to another room. Entering that room, Travis was pleased to see four more "Men" that looked very similar in appearance to the one that lead him to this room. Travis thought one might be a woman, because she had a little longer hair, looked more feminine and was a little shorter than the others. As Travis and his guide approached the others, they saw him, turned and started to put what seemed to be a plastic or clear mask over his face. They did it slow and not menacing, so Travis was not frightened or resist. Next thing Travis remembered is walking on the highway in Heber, Arizona.

It didn't take long for Travis to realize that the people he encountered were most likely not human.

There are many skeptics to this case as one might expect. The appearance on the gameshow "The Moment of Truth" did not help matters. Knowing that the show was supposedly rigged to catch cheating spouses and other shocking revelations for the network's ratings, doesn't really add to the credibility of that lie detector test. Just like politics, people will align with one side or another and given arguments for both sides, people will believe what they want to believe. However, I might add that polygraph testing is not an exact science and the tests can be beat (this is why they are inadmissible in a court of law), the chances of passing 19 polygraphs by a single person, or all 6 crew members passing a polygraph on the incident provided by a State Police examiner (one inconclusive) are a million to one. Polygraphs are mostly reliable, but not in every case.

Another famous case takes place at a U.S. military base in England which has become known as The Rendlesham Forest Incident.

The Rendlesham Forest Incident

The Rendlesham Forest Incident has become England's most celebrated UFO incident and sometimes referred to as "Britain's Roswell." The incident takes place just outside of the dual air NATO bases of RAF Woodbridge and Lakenheath-Bentwaters in Suffolk, England. Rendlesham Forest is really outside of Bentwaters air base. There was a UFO incident at this same location back in 1956, but the more detailed and later one which we will discuss here, is more famous and sometimes referred to as The Bentwaters UFO Case.

The United States Air Force (USAF) was occupying the Bentwaters base at the height of the Soviet invasion of Afghanistan on Dec. 26th, 1980. During the early morning hours on that day, the people who lived in the vicinity of the base reported seeing lighted objects dropping out of the sky. These objects were tracked on radar by the British and American militaries, as well as, civilian radar flight controllers. These objects were also seen by two U.S. Air Force military policeman who thought an aircraft had crash landed just outside of the Rendlesham Forest gate on the Bentwaters base. U.S. Air Force personnel searched the nearby forest for signs of debris, but instead encountered a strange light hovering just above the ground that seemed to react to the patrol by growing in intensity the closer they got to the object. The patrol quickly called-in the report of the object to the air base security division which promptly sent units to the scene.

Two members of the security detail (Burroughs and Penniston) approached the object on foot. One of the men saw that the object had a very smooth glass like surface and he noticed it had strange markings on it; like hieroglyphics. Since these two men were closer than the rest, they noticed that rather than hovering above the ground, the craft was resting upon three landing-gear struts. Sgt. Penniston actually touched the craft and both men reported feeling static electricity all around them for the hairs on their arms and head were rising and tingling. Sgt. Penniston reported having a thought or seeing an image of a series of 1's and o's when he touched the craft. He recorded everything he saw and felt in his hand-held notebook he had with him while investigation. Later, thinking this series of numbers could be a binary computer code, he had it examined by and expert. The results we will get to at the end of this incident.

The landing-gear struts were suddenly retracted and the craft and levitated just above the ground. The object then started to glide over the men's heads, weaving its way through the treetops as it gained altitude. Then all of a sudden, the object shot straight up and out of sight in an instant. The men immediately returned to their headquarters to report the incident.

The UFO's trajectory toward Rendlesham Forest brought it dangerously close to the highly secure air base. The concern of base security was also heightened because radio contact with the patrol sent to investigate the falling object was lost to interference once the truck of personnel had entered the forest near where the object was sighted falling. One of the air base's jets that was scrambled to track the object picked up a heat signature exactly where the patrol encountered the glowing object. The base went on full alert, accordingly. Later that morning after sunrise, a security team went out again to investigate the site. They discovered the landing gear impression left on the ground where they had earlier encountered the craft. Although not at levels dangerous to humans, they also detected higher than normal radiation levels at the site than that of the surrounding area which was deemed normal. This wasn't the end of this incident.

In the late-night hours of the very next day on Dec. 27th, the mystery lights returned. Not believing the report from his men the night before, deputy base commander Lt. Colonel Charles Halt and other officers led separate security teams into Rendlesham Forest to investigate. Lt. Colonel Halt carried with him a hand-held tape recorder which he used to narrate the ongoing investigation which covered the fear in his voice as well as other details. The first security team to reach the glowing object saw that it was changing colors as it floated through the trees. The closer they approached, the thicker a yellow fog became that hung to the forest floor and swirled around the height of the men's knees. When they entered a clearing even closer to the object, the glowing increased in intensity and started floating away from the team. The object stopped and hovered at the top of the tree-line. The team continued until they were almost under it, when the object emitted a pulse of energy. A beam of intense white light that struck the ground not very far from the men's feet. The residual light from the beam enveloped the team. All reported a surge of static electricity in the air, because the hair on the arms stood up and they felt tingling on their head and arms.

This was Lt. Colonel Halt's team and this story of events is well documented and verified.

Supposedly, (could not be corroborated by Lt. Colonel Halt or Sgt. Penniston) another airman reported he was on another security team that night opposite Lt. Colonel Halt. This other team encountered another light that was hovering. The area was cordoned off and portable lights were placed all around the hovering craft. A staff car arrived with senior officers. An orb-like object seemed to emerge from the back of the first object which floated a few feet above the ground. The team was in awe as they observed what seemed to be creatures inside the glowing, floating orb. A witness later testified that the orb with the child-size creatures wearing silvery jumpsuits floated in front of the senior officers and seemed to be communicating with them even though no words were spoken. The senior officers ordered all the personnel to leave the area and search for other lights that were now falling at different areas within the forest.

Lt. Colonel Halt reported that he felt like this incident ruined his career. On the fast track he was trusted with more responsibility early on and made rank quickly. He was warned by his base commander to not file an official report. Lt. Colonel Halt did file a report and stayed true to the events as to the way he saw them. He was never again trusted with more responsibility and given less of a duty assignment after the event and never made rank again. He retired as a Lt. Colonel.

Sgt. Penniston filed his report as he had experienced it and later had the numbered series he had imprinted in his mind when he touched the craft and subsequently wrote in his notebook, analyzed by professional in binary code. He was shocked that the numbers made some sense. Penniston was expecting gibberish, because he wasn't sure if it was binary code. The message read like this:

Exploration of Humanity 666 8100

52.0942532N 13.131269W

Continuous for Planetary ADVAN???

Fourth Coordinate Continuous UQS CbPR BEFORE

16.763177N 89.117768W

34.800272N 111.843567W

29.977836N 31.131649E

14.701505S 75.167043W

36.256845N 117.100632E

37.110195N 25.372281E

Eyes of Your Eyes

Origin 52.0942532N 13.131269W

Origin Year 8100

Penniston also reported being ordered downstairs to one of the rooms in the sublevels of the base a day after his event to debrief with authorized officials. He was escorted and interviewed by two men that were in black suits.

Penniston asked what agency they worked for and was never given an answer. Basically, he was told by these men to forget everything that happened the other night in the forest and to never discuss it with anyone again. Penniston, scared to talk about the incident did just that. He kept quiet until he felt safe to do so years later. He and Burroughs stayed in contact after retirement and both had talked to Lt. Colonel Halt. All three men continue to talk about their experience to this day and have even traveled to see the site of the incident as civilians many years later.

Official military and civilian investigators assumed the what the military personnel saw was the lighthouse beacon some 5 miles away sending it's beam through the trees. That became the official story given to the public even though Penniston, Burroughs and Halt said they knew where the lighthouse was and had seen the light coming from it on many nights throughout their tour of duty at the base. They firmly stated what they saw that night was definitely not the lighthouse beam through the trees.

Despite the witnesses' testimony, the only official documentation on the incident was released over 20 years later by the British Office of Official Secrets which many believe to have been sanitized. Any documentation on the incident from the U.S. is classified and not available. Did aliens really make contact with U.S. service personnel......Or was it a psy-op (psychological operation) by the military to evaluate the response of its personnel to an event IF it were to happen? To this day the incident is still an enigma.

Depictions of UFO Rendelsham Forest Incident

The Phoenix Lights

The case that had come to be known as The Phoenix Lights was a mass UFO sighting and occurred in 1997 over the greater part of the State of Arizona, Nevada, and the Mexican State of Sonora and was witnessed by thousands of people. Some video footage was televised of the incident of some lights appearing and disappearing in the night sky. The UFO was said to be as big as 15 city blocks to a mile across. Witnesses said they got an idea of how big it was because when it flew over their heads, all the stars in the sky were blocked from view leaving just a black blank space. It seemed to be in the shape of a "V" or wedge with lights that were evenly distributed along its body. Governor Fife Symington was a witness to the event and mocked it initially. Later, when he gave in to the multitude of letters received from the public, Symington called for an investigation of the sighting. This did not bode well for his career as a politician. He felt he was forced out of office and made a laughing stock from his peers for giving the incident any credit. The military said some flares were released by a training flight mission of some A-10 thunderbolt 2's. Anyone who investigated this claim found this to be true, but that exercise and flare drop was not at the same place or the same time as the sighting.

(Sidenote: I am a military veteran and have seen and experience flares during exercises. I viewed one of the videos of the Phoenix Lights incident and determined that they were not flares. Flares drop in altitude as they burn and flicker in intensity. These lights stayed in a uniform line and did not flicker.)

There isn't much to tell about this case except it being noticed by thousands of people as it moved northwest to southwest at a very slow rate of speed and made no noise whatsoever. The military denied any radar signatures were captured and said no planes were scrambled to intercept. This flies in the face of the accusations by witnesses saying they saw and heard fighter jets flying in the same direction as the UFO minutes after it had already passed the area where it was witnessed. Like the Rendelsham Forest Incident, this case remains an enigma.

A photo from the Phoenix Lights Incident 1997

There are a ton more cases and many, many people throughout the last 120 years that are of some importance to Ufology. There are too many to list here, but I wanted to cover some of the more important cases to show that not all witnesses to UFO's are of a rural environment with a 6th grade education named "Bubba."

Many witnesses are very educated with common sense and some with high government and military clearances.

The C.I.A. doing its job after the Condon Report discrediting any witnesses cannot be ruled out.

While studying all the cases of UFO's, I was led into other areas such as the Hollow Earth Theory, Secret U.S.

Military Black Projects, and UFO abduction cases. I read everything I could get me hands on that could give me some insight to what is really going on that we are not told and how this would "mesh" with scripture. I read Whitley Streiber's book, "Communion." I read a small library of books on certain topics, keeping most of the books until today as a reference if I ever needed it. I read the books of Budd Hopkins and those of Raymond E. Fowler. Of particular note, I read Fowler's "The Watchers" and "The Watchers II" which at first, I disregarded as too far-fetched to have any sliver of truth to it. However, more than 10 years later, I couldn't look at those books as mere fiction anymore. I started to consider that there could be a lot of truth to them. I had a very tough time rationalizing that there was the existence of extraterrestrial life. How could God allow the alien species of the Greys (typical short spindly bodied with bulbous heads and large almond shaped eyes) to not only exist, but actually abduct humans for whatever clandestine purpose that they have? I was confused but fascinated and wanted to get to the bottom of it if I could.

I looked to scripture for guidance. My faith would waiver from very strong at times to very weak at other times. Going to church and bible studies, I just could not totally discount all of the alien abduction cases I came across. I tried to ignore everything that I was reading as fiction and if I ever was inquisitive, I would sometimes ask a pastor/minister/priest about what they thought of UFO's. The answer I received was usually one of the three:

1) Pray to God about it and ask him for wisdom and understanding.
2) Don't read anything other than the Bible, because the Devil is just trying to confuse you and lead you astray from what God wants you to read in His Word.
3) They are demons; Satan's henchmen. Rebuke everything related with them.

So, I did just that. I prayed about it with no answer. I quit reading any books on the subject and subtopics. I continued working and going to church on Sunday's with my family. I left Executive Protection work and went back into law enforcement. Having previously worked as a police officer in both federal and a municipal agency before venturing into Executive Protection, I now worked for a small department in a northwestern state. I remember having a heart to heart talk with a suspect I arrested for disorderly conduct. While handcuffed in the back of my patrol car, he told me of his problems with his girlfriend and their child. He told me of how he used to go to church but hadn't in some years. I was used to being conned by ex-cons and conmen, so I wasn't a push over. I really believed he was sincere when asking me out of the blue if I thought God would forgive him for his drinking and getting in trouble and walking a path, he knew was leading him away from God. I said I couldn't speak for God, but I'm sure he knew what was in his heart and if he would pray for forgiveness and sin no more, I'm sure he would be forgiven. I prayed with him before I took him to jail.

Try as I might to ignore the UFO cases that I read about and continued to hear about in the news or

now on social media, I just could not persuade myself that there was nothing to it when people of every culture from all over the world describe the same beings, even before the day of modern movies that sensationalize a certain type of being as an alien. Actually, Close Encounters of The Third Kind was supposedly based on a classified incident that took place including the description of the alien beings – the small statured Greys.

With the Greys becoming not just a possibility, but a reality in my mind that they actually exist, how was I going to rationalize this?

Some Greys happen to be taller than the shorter statured ones and seem to have a supervisor or leadership position over the numerous smaller ones according to abduction cases. The drawing below is from Ray Fowler's; "The Watchers."

© Betty Andreasson & Raymond Fowler
The Watcher Greys with Tall Being

Chapter 4

Cliff Notes from Ancient Texts

My belief in God was resolute, but my common sense was telling me that these beings actually exist. I remembered back to what the pastors, ministers, priests and theologian scholars had told me what these beings were – Demons.

In the Bible, one-third of the angels followed Satan and fell from the grace of God. They were charged with watching over mankind and came down from Heaven only to commit and abomination in the eyes of God. They descended upon Mount Herman in Lebanon and subsequently mated with human women. This is covered in scripture from:

Genesis 6, verses 1-4

When man began to multiply on the face of the land and daughters were born to them, 2 the sons of God saw that the daughters of man were attractive, and they took as their wives and that they chose. 3Then the Lord said, "My spirit will not abide in man forever, for he is flesh: his days shall be 120 years." 4The Nephilim were on the Earth in those days, and also afterward, when the sons of God came into the daughters of man and they bore children to them. These were the mighty men who were of old, the men of renown. (Some argue, and I agree, that some of the offspring were Giants.)

These angels, now fallen, were then called Demons. They wanted to corrupt and destroy all of mankind. God granted Satan and his fallen angels (demons) dominion over the Earth and mankind until the Day of Judgement, when Jesus Christ would return to fight the final battle between the good and evil forces and then cast judgement over humanity as well as Satan and his demons. That being said, it would only make sense that the Grey aliens that seem to be involved with the abduction of human beings would be the demons. After all, they were given dominion over Man and Earth. ....or could they also be God's angels? The Bible does not specify if the Angels need a mobile conveyance to get them from point "A" to point "B". We assume that they have heavenly powers and can just instantly materialize wherever they want to; however, the Bible does not say this.

My hunch or feeling that I had to make sense of the existence of the Greys within my religious paradigm was that the Greys were the angels. The problem I had is that they did not look like humans. The Bible was replete with humans encountering God's angels and every encounter with the angels happened with a being that looked human, but yet something about them let the person encountering them know that they were heavenly hosts. Either their physical appearance, their dress, their movements or personality somehow let the person know that something was different about the being than just being human.

An example of this would be when Abraham was camped at Kardesh Barnea in the Negev of the Sinai desert. From inside his tent, Abraham saw three "men" at the entrance. He ran to them and once getting closer to them, only then realizing that they were "above" him. They looked like men, but Abraham knew they were different upon closer inspection. What was it that tipped him off? They were angels of which one of them happened to be "the Lord". (The God of Abraham) This event takes place in the Bible in *Genesis 18 and 19* where these angels are constantly referred to as "men." It only makes sense that Satan's Demons would look like the angels, since both Satan and the Demons were once angels before their fall from grace. Pop culture has embedded in us the image of Satan and his Demons as looking scarily non-human with horns, red or black skin, with bat wings and a tail. Add a pitchfork or trident and a taste for human flesh and suffering. Some of that may be true, yet all of it may be false too.

Still this does not help me when trying to identify these beings known as the Greys. Are they Angels, Demons, both, or perhaps neither and something else entirely? I decided to leave that investigation alone, although never forgetting it by virtually filing it away for future use if I needed to refer to it upon new information that dealt with that topic. I guess what I really wanted to discover is more about God. Why did God ask anyone he interacted with in the Bible a question? If God knew how you would answer that question, why would he ask it in the first place? He wouldn't need ask anything. I was always told that since God knew everything already that he would ask questions of people to illicit a response from them so they themselves would learn a lesson. I was told too that God may ask a question of somebody to spark them to action for a specific purpose in order to answer that question. Perhaps, that happened to me and could be the reason I am writing this book. I wanted to know who God is. I had to find out. Subsequently, I started on a spiritual quest over many years.

I started to look for clues in the places that I was always warned not to ever look – books other than the Bible.

I started to read every holy book I could get my hands on. I read the *"Tibetan Book of the Dead", "The Egyptian Book of the Dead", "The Book of Mormon", "The Book of Enoch", "The Book of Giants", "The Apocrypha", all of the Gnostics books* (there are a lot of them), *"The Qur'an (Koran)", "The Kolbrin Bible",* (not really a Bible - books of ancient Egyptian and Celtic academia), ect. I even read *"The Satanic Bible"* by Anton Levay. These books are not easy reads and took quite a number of years to get through all of them. I figured that reading *"The Satanic Bible"* would help me understand how the enemy of Christians really think. After that book, I read *"The Art of War"* by Sun Tsu. This was the 2nd time in my life that I read *"The Art of War"*.

I then was led to read the supposedly oldest written story (according to modern science at the time) to ever be written down in a complete form - the *"Epic of Gilgamesh."* This, in turn, led me to begin to read a book by Zechariah Sitchin called *"The 12th Planet"*. I began to read the first few chapters, but try as I may, I just could not ignore what it was saying any longer and stopped reading it. I viewed it as so far-fetched I could not keep reading. I think I threw it in the trash.

I gained a lot of knowledge by reading what these books contained (useless knowledge and a waste of time if one would ask my atheist father), and although just reading them and not studying them over a long period like I have the Bible, I still gained some valuable insight in my search for God. After all, when I tried to understand what was driving me to read all of these books, what I was really doing is searching to know more about God. **Who Is God?** I needed to know more than what I had learned from the Bible.

[KJV] Jeremiah 29 verse 13 states:

"And ye shall seek me, and find me, when ye shall search for me with all of your heart."

Examples of what I had learned from some of these books were as follows:

"The Tibetan Book of the Dead"

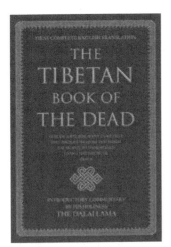 I learned what the Buddhists think what happens when you die and on your way to the afterlife. The afterlife being that you achieve the highest level of enlightenment and reach Nirvana, or not attaining the highest level and then being re-incarnated back to another human body to learn more of the lesson you are supposed to learn before attaining Nirvana. Nirvana was where your soul or spirit or essence merges with the source of energy that created everything. Kind of like we are all pieces of God and when we get to Heaven (if we are worthy) we become one with God. Kind of like we are all one with God but yet separate. Nirvana is described as having a virtually blissful feeling of happiness or

contentment. According the Tibetan Book of the Dead, upon death our spirit goes through a series of tests or levels where you would be tempted to go towards a bright beautiful light, which I envisioned as rays of light shining through a hole in a roof. Because this light is so tempting to go towards and enter its plane, you would hardly notice the dull, barely visible light next to the bright one some distance away from each other. Without training or wisdom, most spirits would definitely enter the bright beautiful light that has a much more tempting allure to it. This in turn would lead back to reincarnation into a mortal human body to live another lifetime. If you are trained and/or wise, you would avoid the tempting light and see and enter the dull uninviting light which then would raise your spirit to a higher level. Once at a higher level this test is repeated with the alluring light meant to instill feelings of greater temptation. If one can avoid the greater light with every test, choosing the dull uninviting light will eventually raise your spirit to the highest level, that being Nirvana.

If you succumb to the particular feeling of temptation and choose the greater light on any level, you will sink to a lower level and then back down to the corporal realm where you will choose another body to incarnate in. If one was evil in one's life, most likely you will be easily tempted towards the greater light and end up back on Earth to live another life. If one had committed some heinous acts of evil and/or selfishness during their life, you could be in danger of reincarnating into an animal body. Since we are all sparks or pieces of "the one" or "the source' (Nirvana), to show kindness to another is to show kindness to yourself. In turn, by hurting another you only end up hurting yourself and your chances of attaining a higher level.

Buddhist monks or family members left alive on Earth can help coach or guide your spirit by chanting (praying) around your dead body to help your spirit along the way. I envision a sporting event or game show where you are participating and your coach/instructor or family are yelling tips that will help you and affect a better outcome.

The Emerald Tablets of Thoth the Atlantean

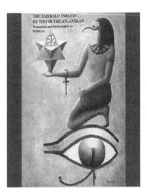

In concurrence with the Tibetan Book of the Dead and other eastern religions, The Emerald Tablets of Thoth tell about the planet Earth as a "prison planet" where our souls are recycled (reincarnation as a human) back into bodies on Earth to keep working every lifetime. We are slaves trapped in this prison. This book tells of Thoth, a priest-king who was in Atlantis and founded a colony of Atlantis known as Egypt. Thoth teaches how to become aware of our own divinity contained in each of us. We each have a spark of the Creator and once aware, we can break free of our soul's prison on Earth and to ascend to be with others like ourselves and the Creator (basically going to Heaven). Thoth says in the Emerald Tablets that there is a spaceship buried under the Sphinx that is intact and can be activated to help humans fight in the final battle that is to come between two factions of gods (extraterrestrials).

Also known as the Smaragdine Tablet, its author is supposed to be the Hellenistic god of Hermes. Hermes was known by the Egyptians as Thoth and by the Sumerians as

Ningdishzidda, a son of Enki. Some authors and researchers of ancient texts think he is also Jesus of Nazareth. The oldest copy discovered was in Arabic and found in Saudi Arabia between the 6th and 8th centuries.

"The Egyptian Book of the Dead"

Egyptians believed that the spirit was made up of 2 or possibly 3 parts. The part that animated the body was the Ka. The part that could travel between "worlds" of the living and the dead was the Ba.   If you were judged worthy by the God Osiris in the afterlife, your spirit would be transformed or transfigured becoming an Akh, or that part that mingled with the Gods. When the Pharaoh's spirit or Ba, left his dead body it would travel east across the Nile River to journey through an underground labyrinth and upon coming to the end of this labyrinth, two heavenly

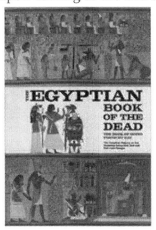

spirits (angels) would accompany the Pharaoh in an ascender (or heavenly boat) to the realm of the Gods (Heaven).   What is interesting to me is although the Pharaoh's Ba has left its mortal body, it seems to embark on a journey that is described physically on the Earth and actually exists. In Egyptian hieroglyphics, the ascender or boat looks a lot like a rocket ship.

It was the only way the Ba could travel between the "worlds" of the living and the dead.

"The Book of Mormon"

The Mormon Church or today known as The Church of

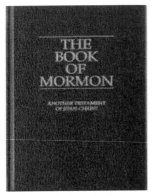

Jesus Christ of Latter-Day Saints, was founded by Joseph Smith Jr. in 1830. His testimony says that he was visited by an angel who looked like a "man" and whose name was Moroni. Moroni told Smith of the existence of brass plates which were inscribed with the lost history of a Jewish group of people who left Jerusalem and sailed to a new land which then blossomed into different civilizations. Moroni told Smith where they were buried and to bury them again after copying their contents to be discovered in the future when the time was right. In the "Book of Mormon" it starts out with God telling Lehi to leave Jerusalem just before the sacking of the city by the Babylonians. Lehi and his sons' families journeyed down off of the coast of the Red Sea. It isn't clear if they went down the eastern side in the Sinai Peninsula or down the western side through Africa to the Horn of Africa before God gave Lehi the plans to build a boat in his dream. He and his sons

build the boat and sail to a new land. The tale is full of drama between the sons of Lehi and their families before and after the journey to the new land.

This land and the great civilizations that arise from his sons' families in the Book of

Mormon can be no other land except the Americas; most notably South and Central America. Later, Jesus appears to the people in this new land after his crucifixion. Also, the Mormons believe that Jesus and Satan are brothers. This was a concept that I found very interesting later in my life when I discovered other books. The angel Moroni instructed Joseph Smith to copy and then rebury the brass plates to be rediscovered in the future when the time was right for it to be revealed. These brass plates to date have never been excavated. The Church of Latter-Day Saints is based on the word of Joseph Smith and therefore rejected by mainstream Christian denominations. The Book of Mormon is considered by the members of the church to be another testament of Jesus Christ in addition to the Bible (Old and New testaments). The book is written as if the angel Mormon is narrating it. Mormon was the father of the angel Moroni who spoke to Joseph Smith. Hence, whey the text is called "The Book of Mormon." (Mainstream Christians, both Protestant and Catholic doctrine does not recognize that angels can reproduce and have children.)

The Book of Enoch was not canonized into the Bible at the Council of Nicea in 325 A.D. Both the Jews and Christians (apart from Ethiopian and Eritrean Christians) do not accept the text as being anything other than theologically

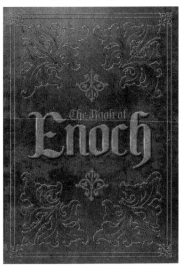

interesting and definitely do not think it was "divinely inspired." It is canonized in the Ethiopian and Eritrean Bibles. The Book of Enoch is the story of the great-grandfather to Noah of the great deluge. It tells of how Enoch was "taken up" by the angels and taught their language and educational methods, mathematics, engineering, ect. The angels were instructed to do this by God. Enoch was shown the different "Heavens" each in succession until he was taken to the "Heaven" where the throne of God was and the dwelling place of the angels. Enoch gave descriptions of everything he saw and encountered. He was then taken back to Earth to write down everything to pass on to his sons so they could in turn tell others. He told his sons that the angels would be coming back for him to take him to Heaven again in a short time while he was still alive. In the Bible, Lamech, father of

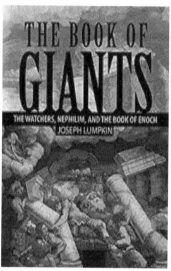

Noah suspected that his wife had given birth to a boy that might be the offspring of one of the angels because of his appearance. Lamech's wife denied she had laid with anybody but him. Still, Lamech had his doubts. Lamech went to his father Methuselah for counsel who then went to his father, Enoch. Enoch told Lamech that he should take Noah as his son for indeed he was. Sometimes in conjunction with the Book of Enoch you will find the "Book of Giants." Enoch was chosen as a kind of middle-man between mankind and God. The Giants or Nephilim that were on the Earth during that time (the resulting offspring between the union of the fallen angels and human women), were known to be exceptionally evil and prone to cannibalism and extreme violence of normal humans. For their sins, God decreed their destruction. When the Giants heard of this, they sought out and asked Enoch to speak on their behalf to God. Enoch did speak on their behalf and pleaded for mercy which they had asked. God subsequently rejected their request. The Giants along with mankind, except for Noah and his family who were saved by building the Ark, were then subsequently all destroyed by the Great Flood. Just as the Bible states, after the allotted time and before the flood, Enoch was taken back up to Heaven by the angels, and presumably still resides.

I found The Book of Enoch compelling and always wondered why it was rejected out of hand so adamantly. I, myself, did not totally discount the words in the book. I mentally filed them away for later reference.

"The Apochrypha"

The Apochrypha is a bulk term to describe booklets that

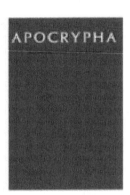

were once part of the Bible. They contain 14 booklets that describe times before the birth of Christ. Some of the books include 1 and 2 Macabees, 1 Esdras, Judith, Tobit, The Wisdom of Solomon, Baruch, Ecclisiasticus, ect. The books of 1 and 2 Macabees deals with the family of Macabees and their struggle for Jewish independence between 167 and 134 BCE. These books were never included in the Hebrew Bible, but were canonized for Christians. In 1534, Martin Luther extracted the books from the Bible that were interspersed and put them at the end of the Old Testament. Since Jesus or the Apostles never referred to them in the Bible, they became unimportant compared to the rest of the Old Testament. Martin Luther thought they had some moral and ethical lessons to be learned from as well as lessons of piety and historical information. During the Protestant movement, many groups omitted the Apochrypha entirely from their Bibles. However, in 1546 they were deemed inspired and are included in the Holy Roman Catholic Bibles in the Old Testament.

"Gnostic Gospels" (The Nag Hammadi texts)

The Gnostic Gospels were not canonized at the Council of Nicea in 325 AD. However, many Christian groups revered these texts as just as important as the ones we have

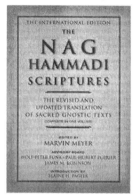 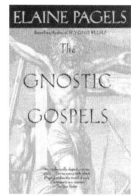

come to know today. Gospels titled, The Gospel of Mary, The Gospel of Judas, The Gospel of Thomas, The Gospel of Philip, Bel and the Dragon, ect. In all there are 52 books of The Nag Hammadi Library.

In 1945 the Gnostic texts were discovered in an Egyptian town just north of Nag Hammadi. They were written in the Coptic language just like the Septuagint which is an early Bible of the one we know today. There are many lessons to be learned by each book, but there are 3 ideas that stand out as contradicting accepted scripture.

> 1. In the **Gospel of Judas**, it is Christ who asks Judas to betray him to the Jewish soldiers. After two thousand years of people using the name "Judas" as a synonym for the word

"traitor," in this gospel, Jesus and Judas are working together.

2.   In the **Infancy of the Gospel of Thomas** (not to be confused with the gnostic text named **The Gospel of Thomas**), it supposedly describes the time when Jesus was a small boy about 5 years old living with his Mary and Joseph. In chapter 3 verse 2-3 a neighbor boy messed up the brook that young Jesus was playing in. Jesus cursed the boy for it saying, "thou shalt be withered up like a tree, and shall not bear leaves, neither fruit, nor root. And straight away that lad withered up wholly." In chapter 4 verse 1, another kid bumps into him and Jesus kills the kid. When the killed kid's parents get angry at Jesus for killing their son, Jesus curses them with blindness. (Chapter 5 verse 1). Joseph then tries to punish Jesus in verse 3 who then retorts, "Vex me not!" After all of this, Jesus decides that all parties have learned their lesson and he brings them all back. Resurrecting the killed child and healing both his parents and the withered-up boy. Jesus states:

"Now let those bear fruit that were barren, and let them see that were blind in heart. I am come from above that I may curse them, and call them to the things that are above, even as he commanded which hath sent me for your sakes. And when the young

89

child ceased speaking, immediately all they were made whole which had come under his curse."
Jesus also fashions 12 birds from clay and was breathing life into them. This is also talked about in the *Qur'an 5: 110*, as well as, the *Toledot Yeshu*. It is also depicted in a work of 14th century paintings known as the **Klosterneuburger Evangelienwerk**.

In this gospel Jesus also resurrects a boy who he and Jesus' brother James and playing with. The boy falls from a roof and dies until Jesus raises him. Other miracles that Jesus does as a boy are carrying water on cloth, lengthening a beam of wood to help Joseph complete constructing a bed, healing his brother James from a poisonous snake bite, healing a boy from an axe wound to his foot, resurrects a boy who died from an illness, and resurrects a man who died in a construction accident.

3. In, **The Gospel of Philip**, the Nag Hammadi text is most famous for alluding to the companion of Jesus was Mary Magdalene.

   "And the companion of the savior is Mary Magdalene. The savior loved her more than all the disciples and used to kiss her often"

   Also, in the Gospel of Philip and argument is made that Jesus could have two fathers. The argument is that why would Jesus pray, "My father who art in Heaven" instead of just saying "My father?" Couple this with that the Bible states that Mary was impregnated by the Holy Spirit or that the Holy Spirit came into her and she became pregnant.

The Holy Spirit has always been referred to as the feminine to Holy Trilogy (God the Father, God the Son, and God the Holy Spirit). Since there are Lesbian undertones associated with that, how can Mary be impregnated by the feminine. To summarize all of this: Mary was always virgin, could not be defiled, and so was not impregnated by the Spirit—not to mention that the Holy Spirit is female, and a *lesbian* divine impregnation is just not believable. Instead, Jesus has two fathers, one in Heaven and one not-in-Heaven, and presumably the not-in-Heaven one is the inseminator, but despite having two fathers, Jesus' mother was still a virgin. I'm glad that is cleared up (sarcasm). I pondered this for quite some time, but now it makes more sense to me after everything I have learned.

The Gospel of Thomas is also interesting because it is a compilation of all of Jesus' sayings and nothing else.

"The Qur'an (Koran)"

By this time in my life Islamic Extremism was becoming household news in the U.S. 9/11 had happened and the U.S. had invaded Afghanistan and Iraq. People would always tell me what was in the Qur'an. I got so sick of people telling me what was in it only to find out that what they were saying was nowhere to be found in the Qur'an. So, I set out to find out for myself. It took me a long time, but I read it cover to cover which was translated into English, of course. I was so moved by it that I tried to assimilate some of the doctrine into my own Christian view, like giving up pork which is forbidden to be consumed or even touched in the Qur'an. Do you know how hard it is to not eat any pork products in the U.S.? (laughing) It is extremely difficult since bacon and sausage are mainstays for breakfast and almost every pizza has peperoni, ham, Canadian bacon, American bacon, or sausage on it (if it tastes any good). That only lasted about a month. Knowing nothing about the Qur'an before I read it, I was surprised to discover how the prophets and patriarchs in the Bible were so highly revered. Muslims actually see the prophets of the Jewish and Protestant Bibles as their own prophets. Many of the same prophets spoken of in the Old Testament or Torah are also mentioned in the Qur'an. Much like the Mormons, the Muslims split off from the Jews in their beliefs because Muslims hold the Qur'an as the last and most sacred text. They believe that their last and holiest prophet was Muhammed who supposedly wrote the Qur'an. Abu Al-Quasim Muhammed was born in Mecca (now in Saudi Arabia) in 570 A.D. He was illiterate and could neither read, nor write. While in a cave, the Archangel Jbril (Gabriel) appeared to him and told him to write down what he said. Muhammed told him he was illiterate. The angel responded by grabbing Muhammed by his throat and choking him. The angel again told him to write down what he said. Muhammed agreed. The angel quit choking him and Muhammed tried to write and was astonished that he could write down whatever

the angel had said. Muslims see this as a miracle.
Muslims believe the Jews had lost their way and
that Muhammed wrote in the Qur'an the true way
to worship Allah (God). They hold against the
Christians the breaking of the 1ˢᵗ commandment,
"Thou Shalt not hold any gods before me."
 By believing that Jesus was the son of God, they
think Christians hold Jesus equal to God and
therefore are breaking that commandment.

One chapter in the Qur'an really intrigued me a

little
more
than
others,
and that
was the
chapter
totally
devoted
to the

Djinn. (various spellings are Jinn, Genie, Jeannie,
ect.) Western culture has gotten hold of the story of
the Djinn and commercialized it. So, today
westerners know of the Djinn by the notion of
Genies. Rub an ancient oil lamp and out pops a
Genie to grant you 3 wishes. I mean, who can
remember the TV series, "I Dream of Jennie" or the
animated movie, Disney's "Aladdin." Although
having unusual powers that might be able to allow
the Djinn to grant a wish to humans, the western
concept is much more light-hearted and

benevolent than the much darker, more malevolent connotation the Djinn have in the Qur'an. The concept of a person being possessed is seen a little different by Muslims. In the west, people can be possessed by a demon or fallen angel such as Satan or one of his minions. In the Qur'an, possession is done by a Djinn, because in Islam angels do not have free will like humans, but the Djinn do; therefore, the angels cannot disobey Allah (God). The Djinn were beings that were created by Allah before mankind, but after the angels and were created by smokeless fire instead of clay like man was. The Djinn were given free will and like man, were created to worship Allah (God). Also, like man, the Djinn were able to procreate and have offspring. However, in Islam, the Djinn are known to not have a body like humans and are formless

 like a ghost. They once inhabited the Earth before man, but because their leader, Iblis, who had the "ear" of the angels, overheard from them that Allah (God) wanted the angels and Djinn to bow down to his new creation, man. Iblis and some Djinn under his command refused to lower himself below mankind because humans were made of clay and the Djinn were made of smokeless fire. God kicked all of the Djinn out of Earth's realm to another realm (not

specified). Just like humans, the Djinn have free will and some worship God, some are indifferent, and some are evil and wish to enter the Earth realm again and do anything they can to bring down mankind in revenge. Hence; all possessions of people are done by the evil Djinn. The evil ones constantly look for ways to get back into the Earth realm to once again claim it from man for themselves. So, the influence of man's downfall does not come from a fallen angel such as Satan, but from Iblis and his evil Djinn.

I found this fascinating because there was nothing like this

mentioned in the Bible. I started to wonder if any portion of the story of the Djinn could be true. Take away the part about them being formless like a spirit and I thought maybe they could be the Grey aliens that have been witnessed by hundreds if not thousands of people worldwide and were talked about earlier in this book. Perhaps? (pause).........Perhaps not?

I next read The Kolbrin Bible, which is not really a Bible, but a bunch of stories and texts divided into two categories: Ancient Egyptian Academia texts and Ancient Celtic texts. The word "Bible" was added later where in earlier times the book was just known as "The Kolbrin." Earlier times as just in 1994 when it was first published. Nobody can authenticate that this book comes from ancient texts or not because we do not have an earlier text to say that it was copied or written from. I learned a few things from this rather large book. Among the many stories, is the one of the Hebrew Exodus from Egypt. It explains why Pharaoh after finally releasing the Hebrews from his enslavement changed his mind and rode after them with his chariots to slaughter them. Never mentioning Moses by name, The Kolbrin says that the leader of the slaves led them out of Egypt after all the Egyptians were giving the slaves gold and silver in return for the slaves to pray to their God to stop the plagues that had befallen Egypt. This is alluded to in the Bible, but firmly stated in The

Kolbrin. The slaves gladly accepted the gold and silver. Given that the slaves numbered to approximately 600,000 or more by scholars, if every slave was given at least some gold or silver and some more than others, this adds up to a King's fortune. The Kolbrin tells of the parting of the Red Sea where the slaves being between two held back waters and Pharaoh's army bearing down on the multitude of people, the men and women of the slave mass started dropping their possessions in order to run to the other side from the oncoming armada. As more and more people started to run, this created an artificial barrier that hindered or blocked the slaves at the rear of the mass of people crossing between the waters, as well as, the thundering Egyptian army. Subsequently, an unspecified number of slaves were slaughtered, unable to traverse this artificial barrier. Those that were not yet slaughtered were caught up in the crashing waters along with Pharaoh's army by the Red Sea. Pharaoh had changed his mind and wanted to slaughter the slaves for their unappreciative release from captivity shown by taking all of the wealth of Egypt with them. The majority of the slaves made it to the other side of the Red Sea to join their leader (Moses).

Another thing of note that I remember in The Kolbrin is during the plagues of Egypt when the slaves were still in captivity, there is mention of what the Egyptians called "The Destroyer." It was described as a fiery red bodied object (assumed celestial) in the sky that followed the path of the Sun during the daytime. It was seen for a number of days, perhaps weeks and then was gone. They called it "The Destroyer" perhaps because of the plagues that they were experiencing and then contributing the cause not to the Hebrew God, but maybe to this object. This would make sense why Pharaoh was so hard-hearted and still would not release the slaves after many of the plagues. The Bible states that God told Moses that He would harden Pharaoh's heart and he still would not release the Hebrews after each plague. Perhaps this "Destroyer" had something to do with this. Did God manipulate and use this "Destroyer" to harden Pharaoh's heart? In the end, The Kolbrin and The Bible concur that Pharaoh and the people of Egypt believed the plagues to be caused by the Hebrew God.

The Kolbrin is made up of 6 Egyptian as well as 5 Celtic stories. What is left of these texts are compiled in what is known as The Kolbrin Bible first published in New Zealand in 1994. Supposedly, Jesus himself read these texts when, as a teenager, he accompanied his rich uncle Joseph of Arimathea to a tin mine that he owned in Britain. There were more texts among the ones that survived, but these were all lost and destroyed by the great fire of Glastonbury Abbey in 1184. Jesus and his rich uncle assumedly chartered passage to Britain on a Phoenician ship. The Bible has no mention of this journey or anything like it; however, it does state that Jesus was entombed in the tomb that was meant for his rich uncle Joseph. The kind of tomb that Jesus was placed in was not a tomb that could be afforded easily. To construct a tomb like that with a huge roll away stone would not have been paid for by a peasant family or even one of middle class. This story of Jesus going to Britain then makes sense, even if it isn't stated in the Bible.

After reading the Kolbrin, I remember being scared to even have anything in print that was associated with Satan or evil. I felt if I consciously had it in my home, I was accepting it and would open myself and anyone in my home to its evil. That's kind of the same reason I refuse to have a 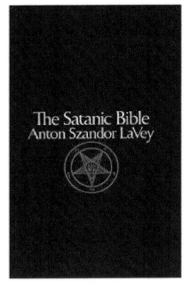 Ouija board in my house to this day. When I decided to overcome the fear mongering, I had been told by others about The Satanic Bible, I decided to read it and did bring the book into my house. I justified it by telling myself it is just a book, and it is. However, I still will not have a Ouija board in my house because I feel like that is a communication device with the dead. It's probably nonsense, but I don't want to take any chances. The Satanic Bible by Anton Levay was published in 1969. There are four books in the Satanic Bible. It is based off of Epicureanism, which was a Greek philosophy stated by Epicurus in 307 BCE. It promoted materialism for oneself that would lead to happiness. However, whereas Epicureanism promoted limiting the gathering of materialism into balance (ok to attain material things for one self, but not too much), The Satanic Bible forgot that golden rule.

I have one word that could sum up the teachings of The Satanic Bible – "Selfishness!" Anton Levay died of pulmonary edema in October of 1997. He said that he talked to Satan every day. His view was that God and Satan didn't really care about mankind except as a chess-piece for their ongoing feud, so it was up to each person to live his life the way they wanted and we were left on our own. Knowing what I know now, I could see where Satanists would see it this way except for one thing – Jesus. I will not go into detail yet to explain this because it will become apparent to the reader as they continue in this book, but I will say this. **"Jesus, whether you think he was a man or a God; or both, would not put himself through the pain and suffering he endured until death just for a lie!"** No man could go through what Jesus went through and not recant if he was a fraud. Jesus did not recant.

The Satanic Church promotes the good that can come out of this religion and not the bad. The result of an action taken when following this religion can be very good and helpful for the innocent, but the intent in one's heart is born of something evil. An example is that if it makes you feel good to give money, goods, or any other charity to children or other organizations, the Satanic Church promotes that you should do it. You are not forced to, but they have taken the Nike brand logo statement of, if it makes you feel good, "Just Do It!" However, if somebody wrongs you in anyway, they do not promote forgiveness or to turn the other cheek like in Christianity. If they wrong you, you can wrong them 10x fold back without feeling any guilt. For they offer a life without guilt - Whatever makes you feel good whether right or wrong, then you should do it.

Some things in this religion which attract the naïve are things like magic. Magic spells and incantations to give you more power than people who don't practice these abominations. However, I was pleasantly disappointed to find out that magic was not what most people think. If a woman is very attractive to men and wants something from them, let's say a woman is interviewing for a job from a male interviewer, the woman would accentuate her looks in any way she could and would bring attention to the desires of that man in order to get what she wanted. Satanists count this example as magic. What you and I call a common day, non-divine occurrence is called magic by Satanic followers. The rituals and spells they conduct are supposed to help them in their endeavors. If a spell doesn't seem to work, then they either did the ritual wrong or their magic powers aren't that strong. It is utter nonsense to me. However, The Satanic Church keeps getting followers every year and under the protection by the government for religious freedom, I think the Satanic church isn't going away anytime soon. If my fellow Christians were ever afraid to look into this taboo subject, I have read it for you and summarized its paradigm. Now you know.

"The Epic of Gilgamesh"

The next book I read on my journey for knowledge is

The Epic of Gilgamesh

A dramatization of the 4000-year-old
Sumerian epic tale

supposed to be a work of fiction. Recognized as a parable or a fable by the first civilization that modern man has written records of and that is the Sumerians. That book is "The Epic of Gilgamesh." For years scholars thought this book was a fable of a mythical king, but in

recent years, Gilgamesh is considered a King who actually existed. The story is still considered a fable though. The Epic of Gilgamesh is the oldest intact written story on planet Earth that man knows of. Estimated to be written around 2100 BCE about King Gilgamesh who ruled Mesopotamia from the city of Uruk (the biblical Erech) approximately between 2800 BCE and 2500 BCE. Some theologians confuse him with Nimrod and the construction of the Tower of Babel in Genesis. Nimrod and the Tower of Babel were located in Babylon, whereas Gilgamesh was King in Uruk. Gilgamesh was considered a giant, for it is written that he was taller than any man living. The reason that scholars now tend to accept that Gilgamesh now existed is that they have excavated the tomb of his full-blooded sister named Nin Puabi or Queen Puabi as well as 1800 other graves at the Royal Tombs of Ur by British archaeologist Leonard Woolley between 1922 and 1934. Gilgamesh was the son of King Lugal-Banda who was half-god and half-man. Gilgamesh's mother was Ninsun (a full-blooded goddess). Therefore, Gilgamesh considered himself a ¾ god. After living his younger years as King, but still an adult, besides declaring that he should have first rights of the bride of any couple marrying under his rule and parading around town at night looking for any such brides to defile, Gilgamesh also saw the death of men both by the sword and by natural aging. Gilgamesh started to ponder if he too, would grow old and die like other men? Still challenging men to fight and defiling their new wives, the gods set out to find Gilgamesh a rival. The god Enki created Enkidu (some kind of biogenic robot) who was a 'wild-man' who ate and drank with the animals of nature who had no fear of Enkidu. To tame Enkidu a prostitute was hired to lure Enkidu to the delights of the flesh and after having delighted in her many days, Enkidu became tame to mankind and was saddened to find out that the animals of the wild were now afraid  of him. Enkidu was charged with challenging Gilgamesh to a fight. Equal in size and strength with Gilgamesh they fought with Enkidu defeating Gilgamesh. Humbling him and giving him his first ever loss, Gilgamesh, respected Enkidu and befriended him. They became best friends and his new friendship seemed to stop Gilgamesh's oppression of his people.

After some time, Gilgamesh began to ponder again if he would grow old and die like other men. Given that he was ¾ a god, he thought surely that would entitle him to the gift of immortality like the gods. After all, Utnapushtim

(Ziasudra in Sumerian and the Biblical Noah) was given the gift of long life from the gods and he was fully a man and no part god. Gilgamesh convinced Enkidu to go with him and they set out in search of the place that the gods went from Earth to Heaven.

The place they set out to was described as east of Uruk (Erech) among the great cedar forest.

(There is an actual place on Earth given the description in the book that could be no other place but Baalbek, Lebanon. That is the place that has a gigantic megalithic platform which the Greeks and Romans both built temples upon when they each had control of that territory. The platform contains the 3 largest stone blocks used in construction on the planet. These 3 stones are called the "Trilathon" and weigh approximately 1100 tons each. Compare that to the Great Pyramid in Egypt which stones on average are 2.5 tons each. With our modern technology and heaviest lifting cranes today, we still could not lift and position those blocks into place.)

Once Gilgamesh and Enkidu made it to the Cedar Forest, Enkidu was able to remember the entrance to the underground abode of the gods. The plan was to gain entrance and ask the god, Enlil, who was the supreme god, if Gilgamesh being ¾ divine could be given transport to Heaven in order to receive immortality and then be returned to Earth. Enlil was already asked if Gilgamesh could be given immortality from a request that his mother, Ninsun (a full-blooded goddess) sent. Enlil denied the request. Enlil, long before even the birth of Gilgamesh had placed a giant biogenic robot near the entrance to the underground facility to guard against mortals coming to the area. This biogenic robot was named Huwawa. Frightened of Huwawa (apparently much larger and more powerful than Gilgamesh and Enkidu), the heroic duo ran from Huwawa only to stop running and face him in combat. The duo killed Huwawa. Because of killing Huwawa and the rejecting of the advances of the goddess Innana (Ishtar, pronounced Easter), Innana pleaded with Enlil to let loose the Bull of Heaven after the dynamic duo. Enlil agreed and let loose the Bull of Heaven from its confines at the underground facility. Both Gilgamesh and Enkidu aided by "magic" boots given to them by the god Utu (Shamash), ran from The Bull of Heaven all the way back to the walls of Uruk before The Bull of Heaven caught up with them. The duo had no choice by to defend themselves. It was Enkidu who delivered the fatal blow to The Bull of Heaven. The brotherly duo thought they were now safe.

Enlil was enraged when The Bull of Heaven was killed. He wanted both Gilgamesh and Enkidu killed. Consoled by Ninsun and Utu, Enlil settled for Enkidu to be banished to the mines in the Abzu (Africa) to work the rest of his life with Gilgamesh being exonerated of any wrong doing. It helped that he was a son of a goddess (Ninsun) and god-child of a god (Utu). Enkidu was to be taken by ship to the mines. Gilgamesh committed to accompany him and then from the mines, set off for the main ascending place of the gods to Heaven (there were only 2). Gilgamesh was undeterred from his quest

to gain immortality. On the sea voyage, Enlil was reminded of what Enkidu had done to Huwawa and The Bull of Heaven. He caused a great storm to rise up and attack the ship. The ship was broken and sank. Gilgamesh tried to save his friend Enkidu from drowning, which he did, but a little-known fact was that Enkidu was created by the god Enki with great size, power, and strength, but could not have a drop of sea water touch his lips. Sea water was like Enkidu's kryptonite to superman. Eventually, Enkidu died of sickness and fever on the shore in Gilgamesh's arms. Gilgamesh mourned his only friend before setting out on foot to traverse the long journey to the ascending place of the gods. Along the way he had to fight two lions at the same time and was victorious, killing them with his bare hands. (The depiction of Gilgamesh holding a lion in each arm is on many clay pots, seals, and tablets excavated all over Mesopotamia.)

To make this long story a little shorter, Gilgamesh makes it to the ascending place and meets Utnapushtim (Ziusudra, the famed Noah from the Bible) who was granted long life along with his wife, but the catch was that they had to live in the place of ascending with the gods. The well that was there was the reason for their long lives. This place was only accessible by an underground entrance and guarded by lesser gods. Gilgamesh was allowed access by denied a trip to be taken to Heaven for immortality. Utnapushtim told Gilgamesh of the plants that grew at the bottom of the well that would give Gilgamesh not immortality like the gods, but long-life. By consuming the plant, Gilgamesh could extend his life many times over than that of a mortal one. Gilgamesh was successful in retrieving the plant from the bottom of the well. He planned on returning to Uruk with plant in hand in order to prepare it correctly in a meal to be consumed, but alas, on the journey home he stopped and bathed in a pool of water leaving his clothes and the bag he carried the plant in on the shore. While bathing a "serpent" came and stole the plant from the bag and made off with it. Gilgamesh was crushed by the loss. On his death bed, Gilgamesh asked his god-father, the god Utu, to implore Enlil one last time to be granted immortality. Enlil denied his request. Gilgamesh died a mortal's death at the age of 120 years.

Scholars believe this to be a fable signifying mankind's obsession for the quest of immortality only to realize that no matter what we do, all of mankind is mortal and must die. The interesting aspect to this story is the revelation that Gilgamesh probably actually existed, as well as the some of the places and terrain mentioned in the story also exist. The mention of the biblical Noah and the "serpent" that stole the life extending plant is also intriguing.

"The Twelfth Planet"

I started to read "The Twelfth Planet by Zechariah Sitchin published first in 1975. As I was reading, Sitchin was talking about cities and spaceports for many flying aircraft in Earth's skies as well as outer space. I was annoyed at first by the claims, but I kept reading on to give it a chance. However, after a few chapters I had had too much and could not bear to keep reading. There is no way I could accept the kind of civilization from both alien gods and mankind on this planet. I mean, today's archaeologists should have an abundance of artifacts by now and would have gotten this to the public, shouldn't they? Even though I had a hunch that UFO/Aliens were somehow connected to God and the angels in my Christian faith, this was going too far and I just would not accept it. I think I threw the copy I had in the garbage. I was angry that I had wasted my time and tried to give it any credibility. I felt like I was onto something, but this book was taking me away from my investigation by swamping me with fictitious, grandiose, claims. I needed to move on. Little did I know that I would one day be picking that book out of the garbage and dusting it off. Not really, it was years before I read the book again, but you get my point.

I went on with my life not finding the answers that I sought. I prayed about it. I continued to go to church with my family. I have and wife and two children. We went to a small church transplant in McKinney, Tx. The church was called Clearview Church and was considered as Freewill Baptist. My wife and I had tried to find a church in the area that we would fit into. We tried the local Catholic church close to us a few times because my wife was baptized catholic and that is what she remembers. We tried a Methodist church as well as a Lutheran, Presbyterian, Baptist, and non-denominational churches. Nothing seemed to fit. Neither of us felt a connection or a sincere love for us being there. Then when we had given up looking for a church to attend on a regular basis, my daughter came home from her grade school and kept talking about church at school. I was half paying attention to her story as kids can go on and on about their day, so I was trying hard to pay attention. Knowing that church is not allowed in the schools, I asked what in the world was she talking about. She told me that her friend (not really a friend, but a boy that liked her which was not reciprocated by her), invited her to church on Sunday at their school. I told her I would look into it. Sure enough, the schools in this district would rent out the use of the gymnasium to any organizations willing to pay for it, including churches. At this time, Clearview was still a church plant and was setting up and tearing down for service every Sunday. We did attend as a family and just loved it. The pastor, his family, and the other people were very loving and welcoming with no pressure. We started to attend on a weekly basis and I would go to the men's Bible study on Thursdays and group bible study on Wednesday's. This was done at the homes of the congregation revolving from one to the next. I would help tear down after service every Sunday. Eventually, the pastor secured the lease of a building to be the permanent home of Clearview Church. I served as an usher and greeter. My children went to the youth club on Tuesday nights. Never had I felt such sincerity of caring from the people of a church.

I would read the Bible and still wonder about intelligent alien life and UFO's. I knew in my heart that there was something to this, but not having the answers or any other leads, I could only speculate to myself. I had started a new position at my employment. This position provided a lot more down time than at my other previous positions with that particular company. This downtime, in turn, allowed me to catch up on some reading. I would read my Bible that I always carried in by backpack to work, but I eventually wanted something else. I thought that reading anything fiction is a waste of my time. As I have gotten older, I don't seem to be entertained if I'm not learning something. I had always had this innate feeling that the Bible and aliens had some kind of connection. The TV show "Ancient Aliens" on the History Channel had been airing for 6 years at this point in my life and it was my favorite show. You have to sift through the information on that show, because not everything on that show sounds likely. However, somethings do. I thought to myself that I should be on that show because I was looking into that stuff many years before it ever aired. I was always hoping I would learn something that I didn't already know. In one episode, they briefly covered the author, investigator, and amateur archaeologist, Zecharia Sitchin and his work with the Sumerian Tablets. I remembered the book of his, "The Twelfth Planet" that I started to read and threw in the garbage some years before. I decided to go to Half Price Books near where I lived and look for books on the UFO phenomena that I hadn't read yet. I came upon one book titled, "The Lost Book of Enki" and discovered that it was written by Zecharia Sitchin. I decided to give him another chance and bought that book. I took that book to work with me not knowing what a life-changing experience that was going to be for me. As I read that book, I started to have an epiphany. After searching all of my life for answers and now in my late 40's, I had hit the proverbial 'pay dirt'. The same stories that were in Genesis in the Bible (story of creation, creation of Man, The Great World Flood, the Tower of Babe, ect.) were in the Sumerian Tablets, but they were much more detailed. I wasn't sure that this wasn't fiction, so I did some researching on the tablets.

Chapter 5

The Stories of the Sumerian Tablets:

A Life Changing Experience

The information that I discovered when I started searching for the Sumerian Tablets was interesting. The term Sumerian Tablets, encompasses all cuneiform clay tablets that have been excavated by archaeologists in the Middle East. Whether they are from the Akkadians, Babylonians, Assyrians, Hittites, Elamites, Persians, Ugarits, ect. civilizations, they were all preceded by the Sumerians in that region, so the term Sumerian Tablets encompasses them all. The cuneiform writing was shared by many of these different civilizations and all were descendants of the Sumerians which modern science has labeled the world's first and oldest civilization. The writing style used wedge shape characters usually impressed onto wet clay that would then harden.

 Linguists and experts in ancient languages contend that this style of writing evolved into many other styles over the centuries, such as Chinese, Japanese, Hebrew and Arabic. By connecting the wedge-shaped characters, you can see where the other styles of writing came from. The cuneiform

writing itself came from an earlier form of hieroglyphic writing that was different from the Egyptians. Some of that writing has been found.

3000 BC	2800 BC	2500 BC	1800BC	600 BC	
					an (god, heaven)
					ki (earth)
					lu (man)
					munus (woman) sal (fine, thin, delicate)
					kur (mountain, land)
					geme (female slave)
					sag (head)
					ka (mouth)
					ninda (bread)

In much the same way, archaeologists think that the writing of many people today is from this cuneiform. The Sumerians are presently the oldest civilization that we have written records for. They introduced many firsts of civilization showing a high development in architecture, agriculture, husbandry, irrigation, mathematics, engineering, economics, law, astronomy, art, pottery, weapons, military and political structure and organization, and of course, religion. They were not limited to just the ones I mentioned. Scientists and archaeologists today cannot explain how mankind went from a level of technology as a group of hunter gatherers living in huts to all of a sudden building great temples and structures that our modern technology would have a difficult time accomplishing today. Not to mention all of the other technological disciplines I listed above. The answer to these questions that modern day science refuses to look at is in the writing of the cuneiform tablets and their religious stories of how the Sumerians learned it all.

Sumerian Tablets first discovered

30,943 Sumerian Tablets were unearthed in the ancient city of Nineveh, Iraq by Austen Henry Layard in 1849 AD in the place that was the site of the Library of Ashurbanipal. Ashurbanipal was the last great king of the Assyrian Empire (668 – 627 BC). The library was in the Palace of King Sennacherib (705 – 681 BC). Austen Henry Layard was a British archaeologist and that is why most of the tablets ended up at the British Museum of London where many still are today. The tablets began to be deciphered over time, from many individuals such as Rawlinson in 1851 to George Smith in 1875 when Smith published his book, "The Chaldean Account of Genesis." The Chaldeans were synonymous with the Sumerians. Since the discovery of the first tablets, there have been discoveries of cuneiform writing all over Mesopotamia including modern day Iran and Turkey. The problem with deciphering all of the tablets from different areas is that the writing is the same, but the languages are not. Much like the English and Spanish languages use the same characters and almost the same enunciation of the characters, the words they form are different. Much of the 30,943 tablets found at Nineveh, Iraq had to do with records of marriages, business sales, property deeds, ship cargo records and the like, but also their religious history.

Most of these discoveries were not really known to the public and stayed in the realm of the academia involved in such matters, as is with new discoveries today. However, with the emergence of the internet these new discoveries are spread much more to the public than in the past, but still not highly publicized. It wasn't until the life of an amateur archaeologist named Zecharia Sitchin and the publication of his books that led to a much broader dissemination to the public of the Sumerian Tablets and Sitchin's translations. His work was a comprehensive study of the Sumerian Tablets and the cuneiform writing. He spent his life deciphering the cuneiform writing and learning for himself what the archaeology was telling him about ancient lost history.

Zecharia Sitchin

Zecharia Sitchin (1920 – 2010 AD) was born on July 11th, 1920 in Baku, Azerbaijan SSR. Of a Jewish family, Zecharia soon moved with his family to the area known as Mandatory Palestine (which became the nation of Israel in 1948). He received a degree in economics from the University of London. He moved to New York in the U.S. in 1952. He worked as an executive for a shipping company, but he started to realize (like many people going through life) that his real passion was in archaeology. While working for this shipping company he taught himself how to read Sumerian cuneiform writing and visited many archaeological sites. Being a Jew, he was brought up on the Torah (Old Testament in the Bible), and was amazed that the Sumerian tablets contained the same stories he had studied in the Torah and more. He logically concluded that the Sumerian tablets, although conflicting in some ways with the Torah, preceded the construction of the Torah and were more detailed, thus being an earlier source of the stories in Genesis. Later as technology improved, some of the tablets were scientifically carbon dated to be around the same age or older than when Abraham (Patriarch of Mankind in the Bible) was even born. This showed that some of the tablets were written after some of the stories in Genesis, but before or at the same time as that of Abraham. Of course, some tablets were carbon dated after the time when Abraham was born.

This is, of course, if you even believe the Torah and subsequently the Bible is actually true. I happen to believe that the stories told in the Bible are indeed true. I have always been enamored with either corroborating or refuting the existence of this truth. The Sumerian Tablets are the proof I was always searching for.

Sitchin published his first book, "The Twelfth Planet" in 1976. He went on to publish 14 books in all in which he claimed only one was a work of fiction. I have read all of his books and the book he mentioned was fiction was his last while he was alive, "The King Who Refused to Die." It was an adaptation of fictionalized characters at the beginning and end of the book that were assimilated to characters in the story of 'The Epic of Gilgamesh.'

The rest of his books he said were non-fiction and were the true interpretations of his translations. Sitchin's books have sold millions worldwide and have been translated into 25 different languages. Sitchin was a highly controversial author.

Many scientists and academics have rejected his work as pseudoscience and pseudohistory. His ideas have been dismissed for flawed methodology and mistranslations as well as false astronomical and scientific claims. Sitchin himself was undeterred by his critics claiming that his work will one day be proven true. He never got to see that day. He died on October 9th, 2010. He was survived by his niece, Janet Sitchin, who helped publish some of his unpublished notes and writings in another book. I have personally spoken with Janet Sitchin and some of the friends of Zecharia via social media. From their faith in the man himself and the honesty in his character they say he had, I don't see him trying to mislead the public in any way.

Zecharia Sitchin

One of Sitchin's translations obstacles from becoming even more popular than what they are, are his critics. One such critic that many Christians use as their source to try and debunk Sitchin is Michael Heiser. Any google search on Sitchin or the Sumerian Tablets will bring up a top headline, "Sitchin Is Wrong!" Matter of fact, I have debated with so many people online, Christians or not, because they always go back to Heiser as their source. Most people dismiss Sitchin and the tablets right away because they have never heard of such a thing. They are new to it and think it sounds crazy. So, they go to the nearest electronic device and do a Google search. Up pop's Heiser. Subsequently, they regurgitate it as their argument. That is about the extent of their research. "I read it on the internet, so it must be true." (laughing)

Michael Heiser received his PhD in the Hebrew Bible and ancient Semitic from the University of Wisconsin – Madison and has written many books on different topics that support the Bible as true and the way the Christian churches teach it today. In my opinion, Heiser has a strong belief in the Bible, the way it was taught to him and subsequently continued his education to reinforce that belief. I was taught the same thing as were 10's of millions of other people. Many more millions are being taught the same thing today. Heiser is not the only critic, but he is the most accredited and most prominent critic of all Ancient Astronaut theorists, but most adamantly, Sitchin. Most likely, because Sitchin's theory and ideas make a lot of sense in addition to being very well researched. Heiser picks apart details of Sitchin's translations and then insulates that since a few details are wrong in his expert opinion, then the whole theory is garbage. For example, Heiser takes aim at the word "Nephilim" in Genesis. Sitchin translates the word "Nephilim" as "those that come down from above or from Heaven". Heiser pokes holes in the translation showing Sitchin is not as good a translator as Heiser is. Heiser shows that to get that proper translation from "to come down", the word would have to be spelled "Nephilim" and not

117

"Nephilim".   Therefore, mistakes like this one and other details make the whole theory hogwash. The bulk of Sitchin's translations are not disputed by him specifically, just details like the one I mentioned. Thereby, He dismisses the whole premise that ancient astronauts could have been the cause of stories of the gods in every civilization, but by different names. When I read Sitchin's work (all of it), it made perfect sense and even if some things are off a little in the translation, the overall premise still makes sense. Remember, it was a journey to get where I am today. I like to think of myself of a healthy skeptic, but still having an open mind.

Heiser has said that at the time of his criticism of Sitchin's work, a lot of time had gone by and we have learned much more about the cuneiform writing and translating it than during the time of Sitchin's research. This is another excuse that he gives for Sitchin making mistakes. Well, sometime has transpired since Heiser wrote that criticism (my research shows the last time was approximately 2012). Today, some six years later in 2018 some more progress has been made on researching the cuneiform writing by more eyes. There are two prominent, well educated people in their fields that agree that Sitchin got it right and that Heiser is wrong!

The first I mention is Mauro Biglino. Mauro Biglino is an Italian scholar of religious studies, author and translator. He translated the Masoretic text which is the authoritative Hebrew and Aramaic text of the Tanakh for Rabbinic Judaism. He was also chosen by the Vatican to be the one who translates the Sumerian Tablets for them. When he completed his work, Mauro Biglino went before a Vatican panel to show them what he had translated. Biglino started to tell them what these tablets said which agreed with Sitchin's findings to his overall premise to be true. Obviously not liking what they were hearing, Biglino was told to stop his presentation and did not get to continue. Biglino is in the process of publishing his books on the subject. His book (which I have read), *"The Book that Will Forever Change Your Ideas about the Bible"* is currently available in English on Amazon Kindle and soon to be printed in English.

The second person I intend to mention is Alessandro Demontis. Alessandro Demontis is an Italian Mechanical and Industrial Engineer who is also a chemist. He happens to be expert linguist in my opinion. I have spoken to him personally and he has studied 7 modern languages plus Etrusca, Sumerian, and Akkadian. He speaks fluent English, Italian and Romanian but has also studied Azeri, Polish, Serbian, German and a bit of Swahili and Ewe. Mr. Demontis has an extensive archive of his translations on the internet even though 90% of it is in Italian. He, too, says Sitchin got it right and it is Heiser who is wrong. Other people who believe Sitchin was right are author Gerald Clark, Matt LaCroix and Dr. Sasha Alex-Lessin who received his PhD in Anthropology from UCLA. These authors have many books that they have written on the cuneiform tablets and Sitchin's work.

Sitchin wasn't the first to translate the cuneiform tablets. Critics like Heiser do not pick on people like Dr. George Smith. He was a famous Assyriologist with a PhD in Anthropology and worked for the British Museum of London. He published his book on his translations of the tablets in 1875. His book is titled, "The Chaldean Account of Genesis." I have read that book and see nothing that would disagree with Sitchin's theory. The overall premise is in agreement between the two. However, Dr. Smith does not say that the gods mentioned in the tablets are extraterrestrials. He merely translated the tablets and published his findings. Many of Dr. Smith's translations are congruent with Sitchin's. Where they differ would be in details such as the name of the god who was heir to the throne of Anu. His name according to Dr. Smith was Elu and according to Sitchin it is Enlil. We are still referring to the same being. The similarity the tablets have to the account of Genesis in the Bible is unmistaken by all people alike. One of two truths have emerged. Either the Tablets are the origin of Genesis and the stories are inspired by those stories in the Tablets, or both texts are written from a much older lost original text. There is no doubt that the cuneiform texts are older than the Bible's writings today. Since the Hebrews were held in captivity by the Babylonians, it would also make sense that the scribes of the Hebrews would have been influenced by the Babylonian religious texts to some degree.

Truly, the critics are correct that there is no way to prove Sitchin was right; however, there is no way they can prove he was completely wrong in his premise either. Regardless of who is right or wrong, nobody can argue that Sitchin does make a compelling argument. Anybody that has read his books would see that he cites 100's of published historians, astronomers, philosophers, chemists, biologists, architects, and scientists of many kinds throughout history to support his theory. From a Christian and biblical standpoint, I find it most compelling and I think Sitchin's theory is truer than not. What Sitchin's books allude to affects the way you would interpret the rest of the Bible moving on from Genesis. So, what does Sitchin's books say about the stories found in Genesis?

The cuneiform tablets tell of the gods who came to Earth. Adhering to the Ancient Astronaut Theory and replace the gods with the words "extraterrestrials" or "aliens", and the story makes a lot of sense. After all, the Bible tells us that God and the Angels are not from this world and that is the exact definition of an alien/extraterrestrial even if you think of them in a spiritual sense instead of just a physical one. In fact, even if they are from a different dimension, they still fit the definition of alien/extraterrestrial.

Although the tablets are much more elaborate and encompassing in the cuneiform texts, I will summarize what they say and how they relate to biblical scripture. The Bible starts out with the story of creation. God created the universe, Heaven and Earth, the plants and animals of the Earth and finally mankind. The Sumerian Tablets have their creation story also. The creation story itself is contained in a text of 7 tablets called the "Enuma Elish". Each day of creation in biblical scripture loosely corresponds to a corresponding tablet. In the Bible there were 6 days of creation by God and the 7th day to rest. Hence, the 7 tablets of creation in the Sumerian Tablets. In the Sumerian Tablets, there were gods that each had a Celestial counterpart. When using the Celestial body counterpart instead of the royal being it corresponded to, the creation of our solar system made much more sense.

The "Enuma Elish" starts out with just the Sun and its 'companion', Mercury in our solar system. I will forego the Sumerian names for the Celestial gods for now. Out from the Sun came a giant watery blob of matter that was expelled to the point of where the asteroid belt is today.

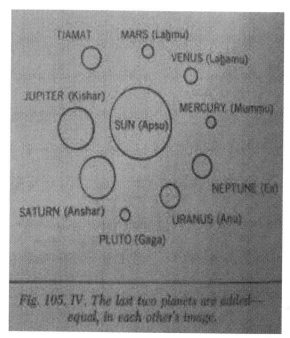

TIAMAT   MARS (Laḫmu)
VENUS (Laḫamu)
JUPITER (Kishar)
MERCURY (Mummu)
SUN (Apsu)
NEPTUNE (Ea)
SATURN (Anshar)   URANUS (Anu)
PLUTO (Gaga)

Fig. 105. IV. The last two planets are added—
equal, in each other's image.

This watery blob eventually coalesced and became the planet **_Tiamat_** who was the mother of the gods with the Sun being the father. Before stabilizing into the planet, out from Tiamat were born 3 sets of twins. The first set were Venus and Mars. The second set were Uranus and Neptune. The third set were the gas giants Saturn and Jupiter. I have known the basic architecture of our solar system most of my life, but never did I realize until I read this that; yes, the planets did seem to be 3 pairs of planets that are roughly the same size to its 'twin' (astronomically speaking). Pluto was actually a moon of Saturn. The solar system was still in chaos and the orbits of these planets were not very stable. A rogue planet a little larger than Uranus, but smaller than Jupiter was drawn it to our solar system by the gravity of Neptune. As it drew closer to the other planets, their gravity acted on it to draw it closer and closer into our solar system. This planet was not on the ecliptic like the other planets. (The 'ecliptic' is the plane that each planet is on when it orbits our Sun. Today, all but

Pluto orbit on the ecliptic in a counterclockwise direction. All the planets today are on the same plane except Pluto, which has a 17-degree incline to the ecliptic). It came in from the direction of the southern hemisphere in correlation with Earth and on a clockwise orbit with a 33-degree incline to the ecliptic. Earth was not created yet. As this rogue planet drew closer to each planet, its own gravity affected the home planets of this system causing them to dislodge matter from their bodies creating moons. Each pass of a planet caused this rogue planet to come further in to our solar system and was almost on a crash course with Tiamat. The Sumerians called this rogue planet, **_Nibiru_**. As Nibiru passed Saturn, it came close enough to expel a moon of Saturn's to an outlying orbit of its own which became, Pluto. This is why Pluto has a 17-degree incline to the ecliptic and rotates clockwise around the Sun; as does Nibiru and many comets. As it came closer to Tiamat, Nibiru's gravity caused Tiamat to sprout 11 moons. The largest moon of Tiamat the Sumerian's called, Kingu. Nibiru and at least its 4 moons came so close to Tiamat as to discharge a static electric current like lightning between the two worlds that split Tiamat almost in two. Tiamat had been cleaved in two, but not completely. After passing Tiamat, Nibiru was now captured by the gravity of our Sun and became a permanent fixture to our system. It is on an oblong orbit like a comet and not like the nearly uniformed oval orbits of the other planets. It comes as close into our solar system as its first pass with Tiamat and then back out into deep space only to return again every 3600 years. It's second orbit brought it close once again to the cleaved Tiamat. This time the affect Nibiru's gravity had on Tiamat finished tearing her in two. The largest of Nibiru's moons called, "The North Wind" in the texts directly collided with one half of the cleaved Tiamat sending that half into a closer orbit with our Sun. The other half of Tiamat that was not struck was torn and crushed by the much larger Nibiru and strung out along the orbit of the once existing Tiamat. The torn and crushed body of Tiamat became the asteroid belt. Some debris in this cosmic collision was thrown out of its normal orbit and became the comets which have very strange orbits of their own which do not line up with the ecliptic. The other half of Tiamat struck by Nibiru's moon, attained a closer orbit to the Sun which became Earth.

*(This theory totally makes sense when you think about the theory that all of the continents today used to fit together like a jigsaw puzzle into one giant landmass called, **Pangea**. Modern science today accepts the one land mass theory of Pangea, but has no accepted or even prevalent theory on the formation of our solar system).*

As the half of Tiamat that eventually became Earth was knocked into a closer orbit with the Sun, its largest 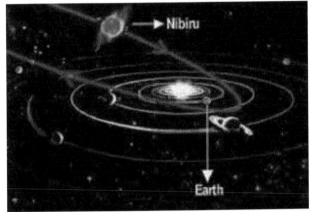 moon, Kingu was pulled by the future Earth and/or expelled by the much larger Nibiru to accompany the future Earth. So, the moon we know today is Tiamat's Kingu. The other ten moons that Tiamat had were crushed and strewn out along with the other half of Tiamat becoming the Asteroid Belt (the Hammered Bracelet by the Sumerians.) This violent interaction of gravitational forces between the aboriginal planets and this invader caused our solar system to form the way it is today. This added stability to the system and Nibiru explains the perturbations seen by all of the planets observed by our modern astronomers.

Today astronomers, Mike Brown and Konstantin Batygin of Caltech University are on the cutting edge of finding a planet in our solar system they call, Planet 9. It would have been called Planet 10 or Planet X, but Pluto was demoted of its planet status in 2006 by the International Astronomical Union (IAU). Mike Brown was largely responsible for the downgraded status and is leading the way with Konstantin for the search for this planet not discovered yet. Brown and Konstantin have mathematically proven that this celestial object exists, yet have no visual confirmation of it, as of yet. The mathematical calculations of Planet 9 by these two astronomers has been accepted by the IAU. As the search continues, this pair of astronomers have determined recently that this Planet 9 must have an orbit approximately 33 degrees inclined to the solar ecliptic. This is exactly what the Sumerians told us 6000+ years ago, according to Sitchin. It seems that modern science continues to catch up to what the archaeology has told us transpired and has already been discovered.

Chapter 6

Creation Stories Between the Bible and Sumerians

The creation of the Universe in scripture roughly equates to the creation of our solar system by the Celestial gods of the Sumerians that we just went over. If we think of the word 'God' in *Genesis 1-2* as the Celestial god of Nibiru it tends to make sense. The 'deep' being space itself and the 'Heavens' being the collection of the other planets, the asteroid belt, and comets. Earth was created by this Celestial event after the collision with Nibiru's moon. Itself being the other half remnant of Tiamat.

Genesis 1-2:

In the beginning, God created the heavens and the Earth. 2 The Earth was without form and void, and darkness was over the face of the deep. And the Spirit of God was hovering over the face of the waters.

The 'waters' mentioned in the beginning of Genesis are the planets themselves. The outer planets being the 'waters above'. The inner planets being the 'waters below'. 'The firmament in between' being the asteroid belt and the planet Nibiru itself, since its orbit crosses our solar ecliptic right at that point where the asteroid belt orbits Hence, why it was called Heaven (Nibiru). Some Bibles replace the word 'firmament' with 'expanse'. All created by one event by a Celestial god.

<u>Genesis 6-8:</u>

6 "And God said, "Let there be an expanse in the midst of the waters, and let it separate the waters from the waters." 7 And God made the expanse and separated the waters that were under the expanse from the waters that were above the expanse. And it was so. 8 And God called the expanse, Heaven. And there was evening and there was morning, the second day.

The Babylonians, of which we have much more evidence than the Sumerians before them, changed the name of Nibiru to the patron god of Babylon, Marduk. The reader might be familiar with a depiction of the Archangel Michael defeating and subduing the 'dragon'. We are told in biblical studies that there was a war in Heaven when Satan and his angels were defeated by the Archangel Michael and cast out of Heaven. Tiamat was known as the great multi-headed dragon (multi-headed form her additional moons). If Marduk was substituted for Nibiru, then indeed, Marduk did defeat Tiamat the great dragon and cast her down (closer to the Sun) not to Earth, but she became Earth (actually just half of her). This war in heaven is depicted in many seals and artwork of the Babylonians as the battle between Marduk and Tiamat.

Marduk vs Tiamat

Notice the uncanny similarity between the depiction of the Archangel Michael vs Satan. (Dragon) and Marduk vs Tiamat (Dragon)

Michael vs Satan

Besides the Celestial gods, the Sumerians had the other class of gods. These gods they called the Anunnaki. Anu being the King of the gods in Heaven (on Nibiru). Anunnaki meaning: "Those who from Heaven came down to Earth." If the reader remembers their biblical stories, at first glance once thinks of the fallen angels. However, there is another story in the cuneiform tablets that tells a tale in detail that would more aptly fit the fallen Angels than this one. We will get to that a little later.

The Anunnaki on Earth

The first of the Anunnaki to arrive on Earth was former King Alalu. The tablets tell us that King Alalu usurped the throne of King Lahma and killed him. Both were of different royal bloodline branches. Anu was the cupbearer of King Alalu and agreed with him that he would not fight him for the throne if the grandson they both shared in common, Marduk, was to succeed Alalu on the throne. Marduk was the son of Enki and Damkina. Enki (given name was Ea) was the son of Anu. He married Damkina; a daughter of Alalu. This did not last and Anu challenged Alalu for the throne and beat him in hand to hand combat, usurping Alalu on the throne. Alalu was in fear for his life and thought that Anu would have him killed, so he hijacked a 'celestial chariot' (spaceship) and fled their home planet. This ship had "weapons of terror" on it. (Nuclear weapons or similar). Alalu fled to a planet he thought would sustain life without the help of their technology. The closest planet that would suffice was Earth. In the past the Anunnaki had trouble getting by the asteroid belt to have access to the inner planets. We are not told why. We are told that Alalu used the 'weapons of terror' to blast holes and a pathway through the asteroid belt (they called it the 'hammered bracelet') to allow him to get his ship to Earth. He touched down in the waters of the Persian Gulf. He soon was able to detect the presence of the monoatomic gold in the water that the Anunnaki needed to repair their atmosphere. This crisis with their atmosphere on Nibiru is what led to Alalu usurping the throne from Lhama to begin with.

130

Alalu thought of a way he could regain the throne from Anu on Nibiru. He thought he could negotiate for himself to be the savior of Nibiru for finding the gold necessary and in exchange he would regain the throne. After all, what happened to Lhama could also happen to Anu if he didn't find a solution to the crisis. When Alalu contacted Nibiru through technological communications to negotiate this, Anu took it into consideration and sent a party of 50 Anunnaki to Earth to confirm Alalu's claim. This party of 50 was led by Anu's first born son, Ea (pronounced Ay-ah). Ea was Anu's first born son, but not the heir to the throne. The title of heir went to Anu's second born son, Enlil. Ea was the offspring of Anu and a concubine, whereas Enlil was the offspring of Anu and his official consort (wife). The Hebrews had the same customs of the blood rite inheritance, just like Abraham's sons of Ishmael and Isaac.

Ea confirmed the presence of the monoatomic gold in the waters on Earth. King Anu charged Ea with setting up a colony to retrieve the gold from the waters. The first city founded by Ea and the Anunnaki was the city of Eridu. Soon other cities were founded: Ur, Nippur, Sippar, Babylon, ect. All of these were in Mesopotamia, or the E.DIN (meaning house or home of the righteous ones). With this mission being entrusted to him, Anu bestowed the title of EN.KI (Lord of Earth) upon Ea. More parties of 50 Anunnaki each were sent to help. The task of extracting the gold from the water failed to produce the multitude that they needed. Anu decided to send his heir, Enlil, to Earth to oversee the project. Enlil was a strict authoritarian and successful administrator. Enki was happy to see his half-brother when he arrived, but also puzzled. Enlil was taking the head leadership of the mission away from him. This is the setting to the stage of the love/hate relationship between the two half-brothers and the two main factions of the Anunnaki. The enmity and wars that later arise between the different factions held the humans as pawns as mankind got caught in between. I am getting ahead of myself, for mankind was not even created until eons later. The tablets tell us the Anunnaki arrived at this time approximately 452,000 years ago. This would put Earth in the last Ice Age with a much narrower band of latitude at the equator that would be hospitable compared to today.

Former King Alalu helped Enki and Enlil with the mission, but was wondering if Anu would keep his word, which he never really agreed to, but considered. King Anu himself had to make a trip to Earth in order to confirm the amount of gold discovered would be sufficient for their needs. King Anu soon arrived. It was determined that the amount of gold needed was not sufficient being taken from the waters. A more drastic plan was needed. Enki detected huge gold deposits in the AB.ZU (Africa). Africa was known as the underworld. A mining operation was now to be underway. Knowing the animosity between his two sons, Anu, Enki, and Enlil drew lots to see who would go back to rule on Nibiru. It was determined at the same time who would oversee the smelting and refining operation in the E.DIN (Mesopotamia) and who would oversee the mining operation in the AB.ZU (southern Africa). Anu was going back to rule Nibiru. Enlil was to oversee the E.DIN and Enki was to oversee the AB.ZU. More specifically, Anu granted Africa and under all the waters to the Enkiites. The Middle East and Asia were given to The Enlilites and the Sinai Peninsula was given to Ninmah. The Sinai was to be a neutral land for the Anunnaki and was off limits to humans. They likewise had no interest in the ice at the poles.

Ninurta guided the descendants of KA.IN to the new world, but the Anunnaki had no interest in it before the flood. The More parties of 50 Anunnaki each were dispatched to Earth for the mining operation. At its peak there were 600 Anunnaki on Earth with others in ships orbiting the planet and another 300 on the way station on Mars.

<u>Side note: I know this sounds like science fiction, but bear with me and keep reading. These stories are written in the cuneiform tablets and are confirmed by modern science to be up to 6000+ years old. These stories are archaeology.</u>

Anu and Alalu argued over the throne again and Alalu challenged Anu to another customary royal fight for supremacy. Both had a blood rite to the throne. Anu again defeated Alalu placing his foot on Alalu's chest and pinning him to the ground. This fight was conducted in the nude. As Anu was letting Alalu up from his defeat, Alalu angered by his defeat, bit off Anu's 'manhood' (genitalia) and swallowed it. Anu did not die from blood loss, but was saved by the Anunnaki advancement in medicine. They convened their ruling body of the Council of 12 (12 tribes of Israel, 12 gates to the new temple in Jerusalem, ect.) The king headed this Council of 12. Some voted for the death penalty for Alalu's crime. Since the swallowing of the genitalia somehow poisoned the Anunnaki (it is not explained why), Anu and others agreed and ruled that Alalu should be exiled to Mars to die. The pilot of Enki named AN.ZU volunteered to accompany Alalu so that he would not die alone. Alalu eventually died on Mars and the great granddaughter of Anu, Innana, found and rescued AN.ZU. AN.ZU was dead, but not for very long. Innana was able to resurrect him with their medical technology. The Anunnaki had this technology and could resurrect people if they were not dead for too long (time unspecified). This was a few hundred thousand years before mankind was 'fashioned' (created). Alalu was entombed between to rocks, but not buried, his face was engraved on the mountain side nearby to mark his grave. This makes me think of the famous 'face on Mars' or other NASA photographs from the Mars rovers that some people think they see faces carved into the rockface. Lately, there is a picture circulating that some people think looks like a giant humanoid skeleton wearing a crown found on the rover pictures. I'm sure that the discoverer of the picture did not know about King Alalu, but quite the coincidence if it is ever proven true.

Sumerian Creation of Man

Enki headed up the mining operation in Africa. Anu went back to Nibiru. Enlil stayed in the E.DIN. We so far have been talking about the royal Anunnaki and not the rank and file. Somebody had to do the hard labor of mining the gold deposits. The tablets say that the 'Iggigi' were made to mine the gold. The Iggigi were also stationed on Mars at the way station. Soon, the labor got to be too much for the Iggigi. Complaining for a time that the work was unbearable, they went on strike and refused to work. Enraged, Enlil came to Africa to talk to Enki about it. While Enlil was there, the Iggigi mutinied and surrounded his dwelling. Enki was empathetic to the Iggigi's concerns. Enlil wanted the leaders of the mutiny put to death. King

Anu was contacted about the mutiny and the Council of 12 was convened once again. The royal Anunnaki and the Iggigi were at an impasse and the entire mission was put at risk. Remember that this mission was imperative to the survival of their home planet.

Enki came to the rescue of the gold mining mission. He stated to the Council of 12 that he could fashion a worker being that would do the work of the Iggigi. Enki said that they would make this creature in "our image and after our likeness." Enlil voted not to allow this. Enlil still wanted the Iggigi involved to be put to death. Enlil reminded the Council that their kind had outlawed slavery eons ago and it wouldn't be right to create a slave race now, nor would it be right to be like 'The Creator" and create a new being. The Anunnaki believed in a being greater than themselves that they called "The Creator." Enki told the Council that the animal already existed and that they would not be creating a new being. That animal was already on Earth and was not created by the Anunnaki. The Anunnaki said that the Earth was like their Nibiru since the Earth was seeded with some of the same DNA from the cosmic collision at the formation of the universe. They felt that primitive man (Homo Erectus or similar) was eventually going to evolve into modern humans and then the Anunnaki over eons. Enki said that all they had to do was to put their 'mark' on the animal in order to fashion a creature that was intelligent enough to follow orders and do the manual labor the Anunnaki did not want to do. A slave, but not fully in slavery – a worker or 'lulu'. Enki was the chief scientist and geneticist of the Anunnaki. Enlil opposed this, but was overruled by his father King Anu and the Council, who empathized with Enki. They were also at an impasse and Enki provided a solution. Without any other options, the Council ruled in favor of Enki's idea – the 'lulu' was to be created. The Iggigi agreed to work the mines until the 'lulu' was abundant enough to replace them. No Iggigi were punished for the mutiny and they went back to work.

Enki was assisted by his half-sister, Ninmah (also Ninhursag), who was the chief medical officer for the mission. Anu was also her father. Also assisting in a more minor role was Enki's son, Ningishzidda. The tablets tell that they couldn't get an embryo to be viable when they took the DNA from the 'seed' of a male Anunnaki and spliced it with the DNA of the selected Earth creature. This end result was then used to create a viable embryo with the egg of the female Earth creature. The 'mixture' was done in a crystal type vessel (petri dish) which was a common utensil that the Anuannaki regularly used in their genetic experiments. They could not get a viable embryo out of the mixture no matter how many times they tried. Puzzled, Enki told Ninmah to create a 'vessel' out of the clay of the Earth to put the 'mixture' in. She did this and they attained a viable embryo.

They placed the viable embryo in a volunteer female Anunnaki, who would bring the offspring to term some 9 months later. Remember, it was probably an honor to bear the being. The survival of their home planet depended on it. The tablets tell that it took many times to get it right (at least 11 times from my count, maybe more). Some of the offspring could not breathe from underdeveloped lungs. Some were stillborn. One had arms too short to feed itself and so on. Each time Enki and Ninmah would try to correct the former genetic mistake that was made until they got it right.

Finally, they achieved a being that would suffice. It was a male and was stunningly similar to the Anunnaki themselves.

Genesis 1:26

Then God said, "Let us make man in our image, after our likeness. And let them have dominion over the fish of the   sea and over the birds of the heavens and over the livestock and over the earth and over every creeping thing that creeps on the earth."

Ninmah was elated to behold what her hands had made. Enki was also proud of his creation. Enki said we shall call him "Adamu" (Adam). His skin was described as a 'deep blood red' (Knowing the color of highly oxygenated blood, that description sounds like what we would call 'black' today). From Adamu's rib, Enki took his 'essence' (DNA) and was able to bring about 14 viable embryos. Enki tweaked the DNA to determine the sex. He created 7 males and 7 females. Each was implanted in a female Anunnaki who all bore the 'lulus'. The Anunnaki rejoiced, especially the Iggigi who were growing weary of the labor they agreed to. It would take some time to have enough lulus to replace all of the Iggigi. The first female became Adamu's wife named Tiamat (after the Celestial god). Tiamat (Eve) was said to have light skin. Nothing was very specific in their descriptions, but more so than what we are told in the Bible.

Genesis 1:27

So, God created man in his own image, in the image of God he created him; male and female he created them.

Genesis 1:21-23

21 So the Lord God caused a deep sleep to fall upon the man., and while he slept took one of his ribs and closed up its place with flesh. 22 And the rib the Lord God had
taken from the man he made into a woman and brought her to the man. 23 Then the man said,

"This at last is bone of my bones and flesh of my flesh; she shall be called Woman, because she was taken out of Man."

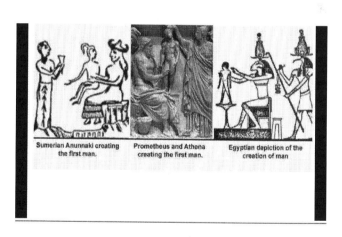

Sumerian Anunnaki creating the first man.   Prometheus and Athena creating the first man.   Egyptian depiction of the creation of man

Notice the size of the first Man compared to the gods. It is unclear if the depiction of Man is of an infant, child, or adult.

Chapter 7

The Tree of Knowledge and the Expulsion of Man from Eden

The story of eating of the fruit of the Tree of Knowledge and the Fall of mankind in the Bible are actually a mash-up of two distinct occurrences in the Sumerian Tablets that happened at different times.

Like every hybrid in nature that is offspring from two different species, Adamu and all those that came after him were sterile and could not sexually reproduce like the Anunnaki. Enlil did not want mankind created in the first place. He definitely wanted to keep the two major things that were different between man and the Anunnaki, away from mankind. This was the Anunnaki's incredibly long-life span (Tree of Life) which was approximately a million years on Nibiru and around 6-8 hundred thousand years if their whole time was spent on Earth. They learned that being on Earth aged them quicker than those that were on Nibiru their whole lives. The other thing that differentiated the Anunnaki from mankind was their ability to sexually reproduce (Tree of Knowledge).

Enki and Ninmah kept producing lulus via the only way they could – by having the female Anunnaki bear them to term. This went on for some time. There still weren't enough humans to replace the Iggigi, but they were being used as workers in all sorts of duties. Some humans were in Africa and some in Mesopotamia. Enki realized that there was no way to efficiently fulfill the number of humans needed for every task, especially in the mines to replace the Iggigi. So, in his patron city of Eridu, he with the help of his son Ningishzidda, tweaked the DNA of some of the humans so they could sexually reproduce naturally on their own. This was the proverbial Tree of Knowledge in story of Genesis in the Bible. For, too "know" somebody biblically was too have sexual relations with them. Enki was surprised to see how fast the humans proliferated. Soon, word got around that the humans could now reproduce. Enlil was furious. He summoned Enki to berate him and discover how this came about. Enki told him that it was necessary to provide the number of humans needed for their mission and that it was not fair to keep asking the female Anunnaki to keep bearing more humans. Enlil, still angry must have empathized with Enki or was overruled by Anu. Enki did not clear this tweak of the human DNA with Enlil, so Enki did this act without the permission of the Commander on Earth of the Anunnaki. The only one to outrank Enki on Earth was Enlil. Subsequently, Enki was not punished, but Enlil did exile all of the humans out of Mesopotamia back to Africa. E.DIN was to be off limits for any human.

Soon, humans were abundant in Africa and the Iggigi were finally replaced. Mankind was not given any rules of marriage and could proliferate with as many partners as they desired. This would take many generations for man, but seemed very quick for the Anunnaki. Subsequently, the Anunnaki in E.DIN would hear of the humans doing all the work in the AB.ZU for the Anunnaki there. The Anunnaki in the E.DIN started to complain to Enlil that they wanted the humans to do their work in Mesopotamia also. Enlil had banished the humans, but relented to the ever-increasing complaints of his people. Enlil ordered the capture (kidnapping) of many humans in Africa to be brought back to Mesopotamia to take over the work of the Anunnaki there.

Enki was always known as the smartest of the Anunnaki. He was also entrusted to be the keeper of the sacred "ME's", which could best be described as computer programs on every aspect of a certain type of technology. These "ME's" would be used to teach a certain technology in founding or bettering a civilization. He was also known to be very promiscuous too. He had numerous sons and daughters. Some from his official wife and many from other female Anunnaki. This was allowed by their customs which started on Nibiru. The wars the Anunnaki had against each other overtime had more than decimated their male population. Laws were enacted to perpetuate their species. Concubines and multiple wives were allowed, but only one first official wife. Enki was standing on a barge making its way down the Euphrates river in E.DIN near his patron city of Eridu, when he saw two human females playing at the water's edge. He saw their naked bodies glistening in the daytime sun because of the water on their skin. Enki became aroused and ended up having sexual relations with both of them. He 'poured his seed' into their wombs. He later found that they had both become pregnant and each gave birth to a baby. One male and one female. Both of the babies looked more like the Anunnaki than the other humans that only had one dose of Anunnaki DNA. These babies had a double dose of DNA; half of it being Enki's.

This result made these babies smarter than the other humans. **This concluded the actual Fall of Mankind.**

The male he named Adapa and the female he named Titi. Adapa had lighter skin than those humans that had come before and was the first 'intelligent' man. As they grew, Adapa and Titi knew that they were naked and covered their nakedness with fig leaves.

<u>Genesis 3:7</u>

<u>Then the eyes of both were open, and they knew that they were naked. And they sewed fig leaves together and made themselves loincloths.</u>

Either by embarrassment or through fear, Enki took the babies and hid them from all the other Anunnaki except for his henchman, Isumud. Perhaps he was afraid of his half-brother Enlil, who might not take kindly to this act that Enki committed. Isumud brought them back to Enki's house at Eridu to be raised as his children by his wife Damkina.

Adapa impressed Enki and Damkina, as well as later to the other Anunnaki. His intelligence was like the Anunnaki and he could learn many things very quickly. Enlil was walking through a garden in E.DIN (Eridu was in this region), when he came upon the young Adapa and Titi and was puzzled why these humans that looked a little different covered themselves with fig leave loincloths. Once he talked to Enki, Enki covered the shame of his act by saying that lo and behold, the humans had evolved on their own. Adapa and Titi had children with each other and it is assumed that they also mated with the more primitive humans. Their children also proliferated and this new type of human became the norm as the DNA was spread to their children. Not long after Enki lied about the humans evolving on their own, he finally confessed to his act and Enlil was not happy. Enlil told Enki that the two things that differentiated the two species were the ability to reproduce like the gods and the long life of the gods had, but Man did not. Enlil, angrily and facetiously said, "Will you give them long life too?"

<u>Genesis 3:22</u>

<u>Then the Lord God said, "Behold, the man has become like one of us in knowing good and evil. Now, lest he reach out his hand and take also of the tree of life and eat, and live forever---"</u>

When one reads Sitchin's work, it seems Enlil looked at humans as a lower form than the Anunnaki and thought the mating between the species was disgusting and an abomination. Enlil himself did not have more than one wife – Ninlil. Ninlil's given name was Sud and she was date raped by Enlil when they first met. The Council exiled Enlil for it and stripped him of all rank and bloodrite, but was soon pardoned when Sud accepted to marry Enlil as his official consort. Enlil stayed loyal to Ninlil and never strayed. (At least, we are not told that he did.) Enlil did not have concubines or other wives. It is my opinion that Enlil looked at the mating with humans and Anunnaki as what we today would think of modern Homo Sapiens mating with more advanced Chimpanzees. This inter-species mating along with the ability to sexually reproduce was the proverbial "eating of the fruit of the Tree of Knowledge" and the "Fall of Mankind."

Sumerian depiction of the Tree of Life

Compare the tree and the formation of the double helix of DNA. Also notice the wings on two of the Anunnaki

Chapter 8

Symbology of the Anunnaki

Symbology is paramount when referring to Sumerian depictions and writing. All of the Anunnaki have their identifiable symbols to certain beings and also, does their planet - Nibiru. Many archaeologists have taken for granted that in depictions of many civilizations the symbol of a winged disk is just the depiction of our Sun. Sitchin theorized that this winged disk is not the symbol for the Sun, but actually a symbol of the Anunnaki home planet of Nibiru. These symbols can be found with depictions in the Sumerian, Akkadian, Assyrian, Babylonian, Hittite, Persian, Indus Valley, Egyptian, Greek, and even the Roman civilizations. You see, Sitchin's theory is that all of the gods of most civilizations that have ever existed are based on the Anunnaki. These civilzations of course had different names for the same beings. Sometimes certain attributes of one Anunnaki would get confused or combined with the attributes of another. In fact, the Abrahamic faiths are no exception. In the Torah, The Bible, The Qur'an, and The Book of Mormon, Sitchin believed that God, Satan, and the angels were all based on the Anunnaki.

(I have also come to believe that this is correct. Even though I struggled with this acceptance for quite a while. There is too much evidence to not come to this conclusion, even if it is just circumstantial.)

In many of these civilizations, the depiction of Nibiru would be the winged disk with a bearded man sitting atop or in the middle of the disk. In some civilizations the man would be absent or replaced with a cross in the center of the disk. In Egypt, the Pharaoh Akhenaten, did away with the pantheon of gods that was traditional and instated the worship of the only god, Aten (symbolized as a rayed disk from above). Again, modern archaeologists are certain that this disk in the sky was just another form of Sun worship. After Akhenaten, Egypt returned to the worship of the traditional pantheon of Egyptian gods. It is interesting to me, given that I am still a Christian, is that another symbol for the planet Nibiru was a crusader cross like that of the Knights Templar. Nibiru was also seen as a star with 12 points or spires. The Sumerians saw Nibiru as the 12th planet in our solar system. They included the Sun and Earth's moon as planets. Knowing this and including Pluto as a planet, Nibiru would be the 12th. In fact, they would depict many planets as stars with different numbered points. Today, we count Earth as the third planet, because we count from the Sun going outward. The Sumerians counted from Nibiru going inward. This would make Earth the 7th planet in the solar system. Hence; Earth is sometimes depicted as a star with 7 points or seven small dots. The Anunnaki who would be identified with a certain Celestial god such as Venus, and it would be depicted as a star with 6 points. Venus was associated with the goddess Innana who was on the Council of 12 and was Enlil's granddaughter.

The Serpent

The most prominent symbology used in the Sumerian Tablets that they have in common with the Bible is the symbol of the 'Serpent'. There is no other figure that is symbolized more as the serpent in the Sumerian Tablets than the Anunnaki god, Enki. I grew up in the church and was always told that the 'serpent' in the garden of Eden was Satan. Now, knowing both the Bible and many other extrabiblical texts including the Sumerian Tablets, I have come to know that is not so. Enki, the serpent, was not Satan. Satan actually better fits Enki's son, Marduk who is represented by the ram. Enki was the serpent in the E.DIN. God in the Genesis story of the garden of Eden was Enlil. The word "serpent" in the English Bible is translated from the Hebrew word "nachash". As with

many Hebrew or Sumerian words, "nachash" has two meanings. It can mean a serpent or snake, but also mean a "knower of secrets". The serpent represents divine wisdom. The serpent symbology is used many times in Genesis. I don't want to give too much away on this topic because I will address this in more detail in a later chapter.

The Bull

The bull represents strength and virility. In the Sumerian Tablets, the Bull first represents Anu, King of the Anunnaki. However, it also represented his heir and son, Enlil. On a more minor scale, it sometimes referred to Enil's son and heir, Ninurta. Ninurta is Enlil's foremost warrior and is the one who first defeated Marduk (Satan) in a war among the Anunnaki on Earth. The similarity between Ninurta in the Sumerian Tablets and the Archangel Michael in the Bible is uncanny. In the Epic of Gilgamesh, the Bull of Heaven was unleashed to chase after and slaughter Gilgamesh and Enkidu. I believe there was a reason that the Hebrews when left alone at the bottom of mount Sinai after Moses went up the mountain to talk to God fashioned a golden calf (young bull) to worship. I believe their ancestors did this practice centuries earlier in Nippur and Ur before moving into the land of Canaan with Abraham and eventually into the hands of the Egyptians for 400 years. The bull is symbolized in many civilization's beliefs. The Egyptians worshipped the Apis Bull. To this day in Hinduism, the cow is a sacred animal. Ninmah or Ninhursag was known to the Egyptians as the goddess Hathor and was represented by a cow. Through the ages, Ninmah is also most likely where we get the word "mom", "mamma", and "mommy". After all, Ninmah was the goddess that helped Enki create mankind. She was also a daughter of King Anu (the Bull) and half-sister to both Enlil (the Bull) and Enki (the Serpent). She was the real mother of Ninurta (the bull) before Enlil married Ninlil. This is why Ninurta is heir to Enlil. His bloodline is most pure from a daughter and son of Anu. Marrying half-siblings was encouraged to keep the bloodline pure, whereas the marrying of full blood siblings was frowned upon or forbidden. (This would make sense as geneticists today have discovered the mutations in the DNA between the interbreeding of full blood siblings.)

The Ram

Marduk (Satan in the Bible) was symbolized by the ram. Marduk is the first-born son of Enki. His mother, Damkina, is the daughter of former King Alalu. His father, Enki, is the son of King Anu. Hence; Marduk has a claim to the throne by blood rite. Plus, Anu agreed with Alalu that Marduk would succeed Alalu before he was usurped. Marduk always felt that his father Enki was cheated out of being heir since he was the first-born son of Anu. However, the rites of succession get complicated and Anu's more pure blood son, his second, became heir. That son was Enlil. The Ram and the constellation of Aries, symbolizes Marduk. The Greek god, Ares, signified the planet Mars. The Romans based their god of war off of the greeks and called that god, Mars. The latin name of Aries comes from the word 'aris', meaning alters. For it was the ram that was one of the first animals to be sacrificed on alters. The ram represents protection, for the ram protected the flock. The ram is a Christian symbol for Christ in the Old Testament. The Anunnaki had a way station on Mars in which Marduk was its royal governor of over 300 Anunnaki stationed there. 200 of which came to Earth for Marduk's wedding. Later, when Marduk gained supremacy on Earth away from Enlil (Just like in the Bible when God granted dominion of the Earth and mankind to Satan until the Day of Judgement), Marduk had the name of the planet Nibiru changed to his name. Since Marduk was and always has been the patron god of Babylon, the Babylonians called this planet, Marduk.

Numerology

Besides symbols, as stated above, numbers too were paramount to the symbology in the Sumerian Tablets, as is in the Bible. The number 12 is very significant in both. There were 12 Celestial gods, 12 planets, 12 Anunnaki on the Royal Council, 12 sons of Jacob that headed the 12 tribes of Israel, 12 gates to the 3rd temple in Jerusalem yet to be built. Jesus had 12 apostles. There are 12 constellations of the zodiac. Studying the significance of numerology in the Bible, one would see that the number 12 symbolizes faith, the church, and divine rule. It represents the perfect governmental foundation and the number 12 is used 187 times in the Bible. The idea that all of the past great civilizations pantheon of gods is based on the Anunnaki of the Sumerians, also adheres to the Greeks. The Greek gods had 12 Olympians who lived on top of Mount Olympus.

As stated earlier, the number 7 and its multiples are also prominently listed. The numbers 7, 70, and 77 are used multiple times. Since Enlil was in top command of the Earth mission, he was associated with Earth and if a figure depicted on a clay tablet had 7 dots above it in the sky, most likely that depiction is meant to be Enlil. Also, the original depiction of the Jewish Menorah candlestick had 7 branches. The Hebrews were ordered by God to march around the city of Jericho 7 times. This hints to Enlil; however, it gets confusing with the other Anunnaki because of quarrels and outright war between certain Anunnaki, as you will see as you read on.

Horns

Horns have always symbolized power and strength throughout history with many civilizations. Many warriors would wear helmets with horns. Both the bull and the ram have horns that they use as weapons for aggression and defense. Horns are mentioned many times in the Bible, as well as in the Sumerian Tablets. Satan had been depicted over time to have at least two horns protruding from either side of his head. Even God's 'alter of burnt offering' had horns on each of its 4 corners that Moses was ordered to construct.

Exodus 27: 1-2 repeated in Exodus 38: 1-2

He made the altar of burnt offering of acacia wood. Five cubits was its length, and five cubits its breadth. I was square and three cubits was its height. 2 He made horns for it on its four corners. Its horns were of one piece with it, and he overlaid it with bronze.

When an animal was sacrificed by the priests (originally Aaron and his sons), the blood of the animal was to be spread on the horns of the alter with Aaron's finger after he

151

and his sons drank the blood. First a bull, then 2 rams were to be sacrificed. The ram's blood was to be poured at the base of the alter and thrown onto the sides of the alter with horns.

<u>Exodus 29: 15-16</u>

<u>Then you shall take one of the rams, and Aaron and his sons shall lay their hands on the head of the ram. 16 And you shall kill the ram and take its blood and throw it against the sides of the alter.</u>

The second ram was to have Aaron and his sons lay their hands on its head and kill it. The laying on of hands could mean to hit the animal or just to put their hands on its head, both probably inducing fear into the animal infusing its blood with adrenaline right before it is killed. This laying hands on the head of both the bull and the rams before killing them is interesting to me, since many Satanists claim to strike fear into human sacrifices right before their killing. Satanists claim this infuses the blood with adrenaline, which subsequently the cult members then drink (partake of).

<u>Exodus 29: 19-20</u>

<u>19 You shall take the other ram, and Aaron and his sons shall lay their hands on the head of the ram. 20 And you shall kill the ram and take part of its blood and put it on the tip of the right ear of Aaron and on the tips of the right</u>

ears of his sons, and on the thumbs of their right hands and on the great toes of their right feet, and throw the rest of the blood against the sides of the altar., and of the anointing oil, and sprinkle it on Aaron and his garments, and on his sons' garments with him.

Three times Aaron and his sons were to "partake of" the blood of these three animals. The ram was to be cut up into pieces the fat separated and both were burned on the altar. This was a sweet aroma to God and was a food sacrifice to him.

In the Sumerian Tablets, all of the Royal Anunnaki wore horns on their ceremonial headdress. The horns symbolized their rank within the royal court. The Anunnaki had a sexagesimal system of counting which we still incorporate a lot today. (360 degrees in a circle, 60 seconds in a minute, 60 minutes in an hour, ect.) Hence; the top Anunnaki of the royals was Anu and given the rank of 60 (6 horns on each side of the headdress). His consort (wife) would have a rank of 55. Enlil was heir and had a rank of 50 (5 horns on each side of headdress). Ninurta also had 50 since he was heir to his father. Enki had 40. Nannar/Sin (Known to the Muslims as Allah was the third son of Enlil and was the patron god of Ur). Nannar had a rank of 30. Utu/Shamash had a rank of 20.

The Eagle

The eagle is another animal that is symbolized throughout the Sumerian Tablets and in the Bible. The eagle bears us up and God is described many times as an eagle bearing mankind up. The eagle is also mentioned in prophecy, such as in Revelations. Moses said to the Hebrews:

Exodus 19:4

"You yourselves have seen what I did to the Egyptians, and how I bore you on eagles' wings and brought you to myself."

Moses also said about God:

Deuteronomy 32:11

"Like and eagle that stirs up its nest, that flutters over its young, out its wings, catching them, bearing them on its pinions."

In the Sumerian Tablets, the eagle is meant as a symbol for Enlil, Ninurta, and Utu. Mostly for Utu and his pilots (eagles). Utu was in charge of the spaceport and all things related to flying of the various air and spacecraft. The angels in the bible are always described as having wings. In fact, in modern theory and art the angels still have wings like that of an eagle or bird. The Anunnaki would have eagle wings attached to their clothing if they were trained in piloting craft. Like a signifying pin on a military uniform, an Anunnaki would be bearing the eagle wings if they had completed their pilot training. This would make sense given the description of angels ascending and descending from Heaven in the vision of Jacob - "Jacob's ladder" (Genesis 28: 10-19).

Many theologians interpret biblical scripture in reference of the eagle in prophecy to that of the United States of America. I tend to think that this is arrogance on the part of American readers. In fact, many coat-of-arms from other countries have the symbolism of the eagle, including Russia (usually thought of as the bear). So, the United States is not the only one.

Now that I have read Sitchin's work as well as other authors on the subject of the Sumerian Tablets, when I read biblical scripture, I am more apt to pick out the meaning of much of the symbology.

Chapter 9

KA.IN (Cain) and AB.EL (Abel), Enoch, plus the Fallen Angels

We pick up comparing the Bible and the Sumerian Tablets next with the story of Cain and Abel. I will assume that the reader already knows the biblical story that Cain murdered his brother Abel with a rock and for punishment for doing so, Cain was banished to the land of Nod that was east of Edin.

In the cuneiform tablets, the story has the sons of Adapa and Titi, KA.IN and AB.EL being taught the skills of agriculture and husbandry respectively. Kain was tutored by Ninurta, son and heir of Enlil, to grow grains for the sustenance of both the gods and man. Abel was tutored by Marduk, son of Enki. Both Marduk and Ninurta by blood, had a claim to the crown of Nibiru. Ninurta was actually in line behind his father, Enlil. Marduk had been promised the crown after former King Alalu, which King Anu had not honored yet. Both Ninurta and Marduk were grandsons of Anu, but only Marduk was a grandson of Anu and Alalu. So, the story in the cuneiform tablets has this background rivalry among these particular Anunnaki, as well as their students.

The tablets describe a time on the Earth when water was growing scarcer (towards the end of the last Ice Age), and the Anunnaki had been on Earth for approximately

300,000 years already and much of that time did not have the animals to eat that were brought to Earth toward the end of that time. Living mainly on fruits (dates) and some grains and fish. The tablets tell of how both wine (grapes) and ale (barley) were brought from Nibiru as were cattle and goats. The water necessary to grow crops, as well as, satiate livestock to continue their existence was always to put the two at odds.

Some interpret the story of Cain and Abel in the Bible as having some homosexual undertones that caused Cain to become enraged, but the tablets seem to push the competition over the same water source as the main factor. KA.IN also felt a little jealous because he thought the Anunnaki favored AB.EL because he nurtured the livestock that was a source of meat for the Anunnaki. The Anunnaki were tired of eating fruits and grains all the time. Regardless of the cause, KA.IN was exiled and was "marked" so everyone would be able to identify his descendants. Being "marked" usually meant some kind of DNA alteration. Ninurta was to guide KA.IN and his people to a land to the east. The question remains: How far east? Some think this "mark" was the inability to grow facial hair. Many Asians, as well as, native Americans (both North and South) have a history of not being able to grow facial hair.

The Bible then totally disregards the lineage of Cain after his exile. The tablets go on to tell of how his people were nomads for a long time until a descendant, oddly enough named ENOCH, founded a city named after him to stop the nomadic wandering of his people. This ENOCH is not to be confused with the Enoch in the lineage of Seth, Cain and Abel's younger brother that the Bible tends to follow, who is the great grandfather of Noah. In fact, there is a city thriving today that has a similarity to the city that was founded by ENOCH. It was originally called, Tenochtitlan. The "T" was a prefix added to many words by the Nahuatl speaking native people of that area. T-enoch-titlan is today called Mexico City. Of course, many people there today have facial hair because of the conquering Spanish who colonized South and Central America millennia later.

Enoch and The Fallen Angels

Switching back over to the Enoch on the lineage side of Seth, Enoch became the man who the angels were ordered by God to teach him all of their ways. Enoch's name in the Sumerian Tablets is EN.KI.ME or Enkime. He was to be taught their language, mathematics, astronomy, ect. He was to learn everything about their knowledge (and technology). This is according to the Book of Enoch which is no longer a part of most Bibles. The Book of Enoch was not added to the Septuagint that the Hebrew Bible comes from, but the book was added by the Ethiopian Orthodox Church to their Bible. That branch of Christianity has 50 million members.

Enoch was "taken up" and taught the angels' knowledge. He was also shown the heavens and taken to the 1st, 2nd, 3rd, 4th, ect. Heavens. Given the description of how the Earth kept shrinking as he was 'taken up', in my opinion, describes each heaven as a different planet in our solar system. The tablets also say that Enoch was taken up and taught the knowledge of the Anunnaki. He was returned to Earth to teach his sons this knowledge and to write his experience down – supposedly the Book of Enoch. Enoch was then taken to Heaven by the angels/Anunnaki, where he resides today. Enoch, as well as, Elijah and Jesus were taken to Heaven alive. According to the tablets and the Epic of Gilgamesh, so too was Ziusudra (Noah) also taken alive and given long life like the Anunnaki. The Bible does not share the long-life story of Noah; however, the Bible does say that Noah lived to be 950 years old.

In the Book of Enoch, Enoch was the middle-man and petitioner of the Giants (Nephilim) that were the offspring of the mating between the fallen angels and human women. This is also briefly touched on in the Bible.

Genesis 6: 1-4

When man began to multiply on the face of the land and daughters were born to them, 2 the sons of God saw that the daughters of man were attractive. And they took as their wives any they chose. 3 Then the Lord said, "My Spirit shall not abide in man forever, for he is flesh; his days shall be 120 years." 4 The Nephilim were on the earth in those days, and also afterward, when the sons of God came in to the daughters of man and they bore children to them.

<u>These were the mighty men who were of old, the men of renown.</u>

This petitioning to God of Enoch on behalf of the Nephilim is also stated in the Book of Giants which is sometimes included with the Book of Enoch.

The Sumerian Tablets are congruent with these

other books, but they seem to go into more detail about the Fallen Angels. Earlier I stated that Marduk was the royal governor to the way station on Mars presiding over 300 other Anunnaki called the Iggigi or 'Watchers'. The tablets tell of how Marduk, who was one of the angels in the Book of Enoch who was ordered to instruct Enoch about their ways, spent time with Enoch and met Enoch's family. Marduk fell in love with a daughter of Enoch named Sarpanit. Later, Marduk asked permission from Anu and Enlil to marry Sarpanit (an earth woman). Enlil did not like the Anunnaki 'mixing' with the daughters of man and considered it an abomination. However, Anu was King and Marduk was his grandson. Anu would only allow the marriage to happen if Marduk was to renounce his claim to the throne of Nibiru and never again could he return to the Anunnaki home planet. This would appease Enlil as well, because no Enkiite (descendants of his half-brother Enki), could then challenge for the throne. This also paved the way for Enlil's son Ninurta to succeed Enlil without a challenger when the time came. The permission to marry Sarpanit (Enoch's daughter) was granted. This was to be the first ever marriage between and Anunnaki and a human.

Preparations were made for this monumental occasion. As guests of the wedding, 200 of the Iggigi that were commanded by Marduk on Mars were coming to see their royal governor betrothed to the human woman. Unknown to everyone that was going to attend, the 200 Iggigi governed by Marduk were envious that their governor was taking a wife of an earth woman. Like sailors at sea for a very long time, they were now going on shore leave. They conspired to kidnap and take human women as wives once they arrived on Earth. It is also unknown if Marduk knew of this conspiracy beforehand or not. The leader of this Iggigi hunting party was named Shemgazaa (Shemjhazza, Shemgaz, other various spellings, ect). So, these Iggigi came down to Earth at the landing place on the platform in Baalbek, Lebanon. (Very close to mount Hermon where the Fallen Angels descended in the Bible) These 200 did just that and kidnapped earth women to take as wives. It should also be noted that this was done without permission from King Anu or Enlil. Enlil was furious.

Marduk went to battle politically for his Iggigi under him and empathized with them. Instead of immediately being executed, they were to suffer the same fate as Marduk and never again be allowed back to Nibiru. One can see the similarities between Marduk and Satan in the Bible. Marduk was always ambitiously scheming to gain supremacy from Enlil over Earth, and maybe one day the throne on Nibiru too. Eventually Marduk did gain supremacy over all the Anunnaki on Earth. That will be explained as you read on.

Chapter 10

The Great Flood (The Atra Hasis)

The great worldwide flood in the Bible is still contested today by many archaeologists and scientists. The hero and patriarch of the story is Noah. When Noah was born, his father Lamech questioned if the baby was fathered by him or if his wife had laid with one of the fallen angels. This is according to the Book of Enoch. It was Noah's appearance that at once alerted Lamech to question. Noah had white skin and blue eyes and when he opened his eyes it seemed to light up the room. Lamech asked his wife if this child was his or was, he one of the Nephilim? His wife assured Lamech that she had laid with nobody but him. Lamech still doubted. He went to his father Methuselah and showed him Noah. Methuselah went in search of his father, Enoch, for the answer. Finding him, Enoch said for Lamech to accept Noah as his son, for he assured him that he was.

According to the Sumerian Tablets, Ziusudra (Noah) was not fathered by Lamech. Ziusudra was fathered by the royal Anunnaki god, Enki. It is unclear if Enki seduced or raped Lamech's wife and she lied to Lamech about the paternity of her son. Another option is that Enki could have disguised himself or took the form of Lamech in order to fool his wife into believing he was Lamech. This option then would accurately cover the statement of Lamech's wife that she did not lie, to the best of her knowledge.

The Bible is vague about the happenings leading up to the Great Flood. It does say that Noah was a righteous man, blameless among his generation and that he 'walked with God.' It goes on to say that God spoke to Noah and told him he was going to flood the earth and destroy all flesh because it had been corrupted and gave him the directions on how to build the Ark and what he should put on it – animals, provisions and his family.

Genesis: 17-22

17 For behold, I will bring a flood of waters upon the earth to destroy all flesh in which is the breath of life under heaven. Everything that is on the earth shall die. 18 But I will establish my covenant with you, and you shall come into the ark, you, your sons, your wife, and your sons' wives with you. 19 And of every living all flesh, you shall bring two of every sort into the ark to keep them alive with you. They shall be male and female. 20 Of the birds, according to their kinds, and of the animals, according to their kinds, of every creeping thing of the ground, according to its kind, two of every sort shall come into you to keep them alive. 21 Also take with you every sort of food that is eaten, and store it up. It shall serve as food for you and for them. 22 Noah did this; he did all that God commanded him.

Critics of the Bible story have always contended that it is impossible to build a watercraft so large as to accommodate two of all the animals in existence plus enough food for all of them and Noah's family. For indeed this is true. Those with faith say it is true without the need

for a logical explanation. This never settled well with me....
ever.

The tablets tell of how Enlil was sick of the younger male Anunnaki conjoining with human women and causing mankind to be corrupted. In layman's terms, the original DNA sequencing for mankind had been corrupted and that most of mankind had many genes of the Anunnaki. Besides holding the young Anunnaki males responsible for this, Enlil also held mankind in contempt for these acts. Enlil tried to end mankind with famine and pestilence before the flood. Thwarted every time by both the resilience of man and by the help of Enki himself. When Enlil tried famine, Enki retorted with teaching mankind about irrigation and fishing out at deep sea. When Enlil tried pestilence and disease, Enki came back with teaching man medicinal herbs. Always Enki did this without Enlil's permission. Truly, only Enki could get away with this as Enlil would have surely had anyone else executed or banished. Still, the famine and pestilence took its toll on man (perhaps due to 'natural' global warming). Mankind leading up to the flood was becoming cannibalistic. Mothers would eat their young to survive. Anyone who succumbed was eaten by the others.

The chance for Enlil to do away with the Nephilim and mankind alike came about when the Anunnaki learned about the next passing of Nibiru. They learned when it would pass it would cause a great calamity on Earth. Nibiru's passing would cause the miles high ice on top of Antarctic shelf to be pulled into the ocean causing a world-wide flood. The Anunnaki were powerful and obviously technologically advanced, but they could not stop this planetary scale calamity from happening. Nibiru would logically pull asteroids and meteors in its wake as it crossed the solar ecliptic and some of that debris, in addition, may have had a trajectory on a collision course with Earth showing up much later than the passing of the giant planet. Indeed, this seems to fit the evidence coming out of the archaeological site of Gobekli Tepe in Turkey. Gobekli Tepe is now the oldest archaeological site corroborated by modern science to be approximately 12,000 years old. Scientists say it could take another 150 years before they have fully excavated the site. The evidence there according to Graham Hancock, is that there were two floods. One larger that was earlier than the second and separated by approximately 1000 years. The second flood on a lesser scale, but still huge was caused by a meteor(s). Graham Hancock's research at the ancient earth pits in Nebraska and North Carolina points to a meteor(s) hitting the ice in the arctic at the end of the last Ice Age and the ice debris that would have been kicked up would come down further south. Hancock proposes this is what happened and that the pits in the earth in those two U.S. states were caused by the ice debris. The ice eventually melted and the pits were left.

Enlil decided to use this catastrophe to his advantage. He decried that nobody but other Anunnaki should know about the coming deluge. Both the Nephilim and mankind were not to be told and would perish from the face of the Earth. The Anunnaki would ascend in their 'sky chambers' to the 'celestial chariots' to await the ending of the flood. The Anunnaki who had human wives could not bring their wives or their children (some were the Nephilim) with them. If those Anunnaki chose too, they could stay with their families and told to seek out high mountain peaks. Apparently, not all humans or Nephilim died in the great flood. The tablets say a few survived upon great mountains. This would explain why there are ancient people in the Americas before mankind was able to traverse the oceans. This would also explain why the Nephilim were said to be on the earth during the time before the flood and also after that. Hence; the sons of Anak in the Bible who were giants (Nephilim). The Anakim were the sons of Anak in the Bible who dominated the land before the great flood.

<u>Deuteronomy 9: 1-3</u>

"<u>Hear, oh Israel: you are to cross over the Jordan today, to go in to dispossess nations greater and mightier than yourselves, cities great and fortified up to heaven, 2 a people great and tall, the sons of the Anakim, whom you know, and of whom you have heard it said, 'Who can stand before the sons of Anak?' 3 Know therefore today that he who goes over before you as a consuming fire is the LORD your God. He will destroy them and subdue them before you. So, you shall drive them out and make them perish quickly, as the LORD has promised you.</u>"

The Anakim and the sons of Anak are mentioned many more times in scripture.

Enki, Ninmah, and many Anunnaki did not want the humans to perish, but Enlil was supreme on Earth. The others had no choice but to obey or suffer the wrath of Enlil. According to the tablets, Enki was asleep in his bed in Eridu when a being named Galzu came to him in a dream. Galzu is only mentioned twice in all of the tablets we know of.

Once in a corporeal form as an Anunnaki messenger in a celestial chariot supposedly sent to Enlil with a message from King Anu to not return to Nibiru or the effects of living on Earth would kill them if they returned. The message had Anu's official seal as well. Once King Anu visited Earth in person and was told of this messenger named Galzu, Anu told Enlil that he had not sent any messenger and the differences in health from the transition from Earth to Nibiru were traumatic, but soon healed by their medical technology. Anu took it as a message from the Creator that the Anunnaki were to stay on Earth for a while.

The second time Galzu is mentioned is in Enki's dream. Galzu is standing at the foot of Enki's bed with a tablet of lapis lazuli (a purple gem like tablet). He instructs Enki to tell his son, King Ziusudra of Shurrupak, to build a submersible Ark (a boat that could survive being temporarily submerged). This would let Ziusudra and his family to survive the great deluge. The directions and dimensions to build the Ark were on the tablet of lapis lazuli. Enki protested that his bother Enlil made him swear an oath that he would not tell any human. He could not break the oath. Galzu told Enki to not reveal himself to Ziusudra, but talk to the wall from the other side of his bed chamber and not to him directly. Ziusudra will overhear what Enki is saying. Enki then woke up from his dream with Galzu nowhere to be seen. Thinking it was just a dream, he discounted the event and groggily sat up in bed. When he stood to get up, his foot hit something. Enki looked down to discover the tablet of lapis lazuli Galzu was holding in his dream. Yes, the directions for the Ark were on it.

Enki did what Galzu had told him. Ziusudra heard the directions and wrote them down. Ziusudra was a worshiper of Enki, but Shurrupak was in Enlil's territory in the middle east and was the patron city of Ninmah. It was the medical center of the Anunnaki. Ziusudra told his people that Enlil would lift the famine and pestilence that was plaguing them if Ziusudra would build an Ark and sail to his Lord Enki's domain in Africa. The people desperate to have the plagues eased, helped Ziusudra build the Ark. This is how it was done in only 7 days between when he was told about the flood and when the Ark had to be completed. He was not allowed to tell anyone of the upcoming catastrophe.

What the Bible does not mention, but the Sumerian Tablet do, is that a pilot was to join Ziusudra and his family upon the Ark. This pilot was a son of Enki's. A full blood Anunnaki that would pilot the Ark to Mount Ararat after the waters began to subside. Only the Anunnaki would have this knowledge because the stars were now in a different alignment (hinting to the tilting of Earth's axis or a pole shift or both). In his possession was a wooden chest filled with the 'essence' of every animal and plant on the face of the planet. This 'essence' according to many, is the DNA of each species. It was collected by the Anunnaki before the flood. There were animals on the Ark, but for food to survive the long journey and not two live animals of every species on Earth.

Ziusudra did what he had heard from his lord behind the wall. The bible and the tablets are pretty similar in what happened during the journey and the sending of the birds to see if land had appeared. Both say that when Ziusudra (Noah) arrived at Ararat, he built an altar and made sacrifices to the God(s). The tablets go on to say that Enlil came down from his celestial chariot and once landed, smelled the sweet aroma for burning meat. Following the aroma, Enlil was furious to discover that somebody had broken their oath and told some humans of the flood and saved them. Once he found out is was his brother Enki, he tried to kill him with his bare hands. Enlil was held back by other Anunnaki and Ninmah and Enki's sons pleaded with Enlil to have mercy, for they convinced Enlil that the Anunnaki could not now survive on Earth without humans to serve them.

Chapter 11

Post Flood, Tower of Babel, Abraham, Sodom and Gomorrah

King Anu later made a trip to Earth to survey the damage done. Everything that was built was now gone under a mile of mud and silt from the flood. Cities around the world were now gone. The only thing left intact was the great platform of the landing place in Baalbek, Lebanon. Anu told the Anunnaki on Earth that Nibiru's passing also stripped Mars of its thin atmosphere and was no longer hospitable for a way station. It was subsequently abandoned. Anu also said damage was also done on Nibiru, but they were better prepared for any catastrophe there. Enlil told his father Anu that Enki had broken his oath, even though Enlil agreed that some humans were needed by the Anunnaki for their colonization. Enki told his father Anu and Enlil about the dream and appearance of Galzu. King Anu took the dream seriously and as a sign from the Creator that the whole time the Anunnaki were on Earth, they were being manipulated by the Creator and that the creation and saving of mankind from the flood was no accident. This was a sign that the humans should live. Anu ordered that the Anunnaki should teach man different aspects of civilization for some time and when the time was right, the Anunnaki should leave Earth to the humans (The amount of time was never specified). Enlil took Ziusudra and his wife to Nibiru and granted them long life like the gods, but returned them to Earth to live their lives. The Bible omits this part, but does say that Noah 'walked with God'. Cities were rebuilt over the sites of the original ones. New cities were also built, as were temples for the gods (Anunnaki) to live in. A priesthood was set up to be the intermediaries between the Anunnaki and mankind. Only the high priest would be able to be in the presence of their god.

The Anunnaki needed a new spaceport, because theirs at Sippar was destroyed in the flood along with everything else. The Anunnaki laid out their cities on a geographical grid pattern. Using the twin peaks of Mount Ararat as their focal point. Their landing corridor for incoming ships was at a 45-degree angle. All of their cities were built at the specific sites to fit in this geographical grid pattern. Enlil's patron city of Nippur served as "mission control" and contained the "bond heaven-earth". Now that Sippar was gone, they needed a new site for the spaceport. That site was in the middle of the Sinai Peninsula. They built it there. Still using Mount Ararat as their focal point, the point of their eastern border were the peaks of Mount Katherine and Mount Moshe at the tip of the Sinai Peninsula. If you draw a line from those peaks to Mount Ararat and then back at a 45-degree angle to the west it doesn't intersect with any mountain peaks and went through Egypt. So, the Anunnaki decided to build artificial twin mountain peaks as a western border point. Enki's son, Ningishzidda (Thoth to the Egyptians) designed and had the Great Pyramid built along with its companion immediately after the Great Flood to serve this purpose as the western most marker. The Egyptians later built around the Pyramids and Giza. The tablets do not say if human labor was used in this endeavor or not. The Great Pyramid had other functions that are alluded to, but its primary reason was for the western most marker for the landing corridor. Based on this grid pattern, they needed a new 'mission control' since Nippur was buried and gone. The site of this 'mission control' was Jerusalem. More precisely, the Temple mount. The Anunnaki had it built as well, and it will serve as 'mission control' when they return again.

Indeed, many groups of men that follow their individual god are fighting over control of Jerusalem, and specifically the Temple Mount, currently today. The Anunnaki also built Jericho which they later abandoned and it was taken over by men.

None of this rebuilding would be necessary if they did not have access to their original mission of finding and collecting the gold that was necessary. The Great Flood had destroyed the mines in Africa. However, the Anunnaki had discovered that the flood had opened up huge "veins" of gold and other precious metals over in the New World in South America. That is where they started to mine the gold. This was overseen most likely by Ishkur (Adad) and Ninurta, sons of Enlil. Ishkur was the creator god Viracocha of the Inca. Ningdishzidda seemed to rule over the Aztecs and Mayan areas in Central America and Mexico, bringing both African (Olmecs) and bearded men with him from Africa. Ningdishzidda was ousted by his older brother Marduk from ruling of Africa when Marduk came back from exile as punishment for the military clashes he was responsible for against Enlilite territories. Marduk was a constant thorn in the side of the Enlilites.

Marduk kept challenging Enlil for supremacy on Earth. He started a couple wars that with the Enlilites trying to take territories from them. These beings would influence the priests, prophets and Kings to go to war with other kingdoms of men that were ruled over by other Anunnaki. Marduk was also responsible for the death of his younger brother Dumuzi. Marduk sent agents for Dumuzi to arrest him for trying to marry an Enlilite, Innana. Dumuzi accidentally fell onto rocks below a waterfall and was swept away by the running water. The Anunnaki could resurrect if the deceased was not dead too long, but it was a very long time until they discovered the body of Dumuzi. Enkiites and Enlilites both mourned. Innana was also called the goddess Ishtar and from that time forward always had a hatred for Marduk. Innana was not a saint herself. Known to be ruthless and self-serving, she bedded many Anunnaki and men alike after the loss of Dumuzi. She was prone to slaughter many men as well. She was worshiped by the Romans as the goddess Venus and the Greeks as Aphrodite.

One time, Marduk was pushing forward with his armies and sent his son Nabu to the land of Canaan to preach and gain converts to worship Marduk as the supreme god over Enlil and others. The land of Sumer and the Sumerians is called the Kingdom of Shinar in the Bible and its people called the Chaldeans. This started a war that is mentioned in the Bible as the War of the Kings.

Genesis 14: 1-4

In the days of Amraphel king of Shinar, Arioch king of Ellasar, Chedorlaomer king of Elam, and Tidal king of Goiim, 2 these kings made war with Bera king of Sodom, Birsha king of Gomorrah, Shinab king of Admah, Shemeber king of zeboiim, and the king of Bela (that is Zoar). 3 And all these joined forces in the Valley of Siddim (that is, the Salt Sea). 4 Twelve years they served Chedorlaomer, but in the thirteenth year they rebelled.

It was 4 kings from the regions that would be in Iraq, Iran, and a small part of Turkey today against 5 kings in the land of Canaan. Remember, Marduk and the Enkiites controlled Africa. Enlil and the Enlilites controlled the middle east including Canaan. Marduk's son Nabu was successful in gaining converts to worship Marduk as the supreme god in these five city states and rebel against the kings they paid homage too. Hence; why these cities were full of sin and had to be punished by God. These Canaanite cities lost that war and Abram's nephew, Lot, was taken captive when the cities were sacked.

Genesis 14: 10-12

10 Now the Valley of Siddim was full of bitumen pits, and as the kings of Sodom and Gomorrah fled, some fell into them, and the rest fled to the hill country. 11 So the enemy took all the possessions of Sodom and Gomorrah, and all their provisions, and went their way. 12 They also took Lot, the son of Abram's brother, who was dwelling in Sodom, and his possessions, and went their way.

Abraham (Abram) subsequently, attacked what was left of the raiding party and rescued Lot.

This brings us to the part in the Sumerian Tablets, as well as, Genesis in the Bible about the story of Abraham. But before we compare what the Bible and the Sumerian Tablets say about him, let us cover what they both say about the Tower of Babel.

Tower of Babel

    In Genesis, the Bible tells us that the people all spoke one language on the earth and the people migrated east and found a plain in the land of Shinar (Sumer). They built a tower out of bricks, so high as to reach the heavens. God did not approve of this endeavor and spread the people out among the Earth and confused their languages so they would not be able to communicate with each other in order so they would not achieve great things.

Genesis 11: 1-9

Now the whole earth had one language and the same words. 2 And as people migrated from the east, they found a plain in the land of Shinar and settled there. 3 And they said to one another, "Come, let us make bricks, and burn them thoroughly." And they had brick for stone, and bitumen for mortar. 4 Then they said, "Come, let us build ourselves a city and a tower with its top in the heavens, and let us make a name for ourselves, lest we be dispersed over the face of the whole earth." 5 And the LORD came down to see the city and the tower, which the children of man had built. 6 And the LORD said, "Behold, they are one people, and they have all one language, and this is only the beginning of what they will do. And nothing they will propose to do will be impossible for them. 7 Come, let us go down and there confuse their language, so that they may not understand one another's speech." 8 So the LORD dispersed them from there over the face of all the earth, and they left off building the city. 9 Therefore its name was called Babel, because there the LORD confused the language of all the earth. And from there the LORD dispersed them over the face of all the earth.

Compare that to the Sumerian Tablets that I summarize here. Marduk was the god of the people who moved into the plain of Shinar and the Anunnaki had taught them the technology of building bricks, because before this, the people were building with stone. Marduk wished to achieve more power among the Anunnaki and thought that he could have humans build a city with a tower that's purpose was either a launch tower for his spaceship

(Sitchin proposes this), or possibly contained a stargate or space portal (another possible proposal). It also could have been just a really tall temple that was taller and more grandiose than the temple of Enlil in Nippur; therefore, impressing arriving Anunnaki showing that maybe Marduk was supreme to Enlil. Enlil would not have liked that. Jealousy on the part of Enlil always had him on the lookout for Marduk who was always wanting to usurp his authority. Marduk commanded a large following of Anunnaki that still believed that his bloodline on Alalu's side was the true ruling bloodline.

The Bible tells us that Abraham (born as Abram) was from Ur and lived with his father Terah. Terah took his family including his son Abram and moved to the city of Harran. It was in Harran that God spoke to him to go into the land of Canaan. The Sumerian Tablets tell us that Abram was born in Nippur where his father and his father before him all were from a long line of high priests in Nippur. Nippur was the patron city of Enlil. It was 'mission control' for the Earth mission and was the religious center for Sumer. However, there were other temples dedicated to other Anunnaki gods in Nippur besides Enlil's.

According to the tablets, Terah was sent to Ur to serve in a temple there when Abram was just 10 years old. Ur was the patron city of Nannar/Sin (known as Allah to the Muslims and he was Enlil's second born Son, but his first son with his official consort Ninlil/Sud). When Abram was 27 years old, the King Um-Shammu was killed in battle. Because of this it is assumed that the political climate would now drastically change in Ur and Terah's family was not safe. They moved to Haran at that time. There in Haran Abram lived until 48 years later at the age of 75, God spoke to Abram and told him to go into the land of Canaan. It is known in history as well as in the Bible that the priesthood was handed down from father to son within the family of the priesthood. Abram was of this bloodline. Not only would Abram have been given a better education than others, his family would have been wealthy and he would have received tutelage in the arts of warfare. Haran was within the area of the mighty Hittite Empire and their cavalry and leadership was feared and envied. Abram most likely would have be trained in these skills.

Another little fact of note is that, Marduk the royal Anunnaki prince, happened to be in Haran at the same time as Abram. Marduk was finishing up another punishment he was sentenced to by the Council of 12. He was in exile for 70 years before he could return to his patron city of Babylon or to his kingdom in Africa.

Abram did what God (whoever that was in the Sumerian account) told him and rounded up his family and servants and went into the land of Canaan. After going to Egypt to get provisions and most likely, calvalry as well, for his family and the men that accompanied him, the group eventually camped outside of Hebron. The Sumerian Tablets say he was camped outside of Kadesh-Barnea in the Negev. Both sites are not far from each other. This is where he staged the attack on the 4 kings that were the victors in the "War of the Kings" in Genesis 14. This is where Abram set off from to retrieve his nephew Lot who was taken captive. In the Sumerian Tablets, the 4 Kings defeated the 5 Kings of Canaan and were headed south into the Negev, but turned around when they came upon the encampment of Abram. Sitchin alludes to the sight of the cavalry that Abram had with him that turned the 4 Kings around, or they would most likely have continued on their pillaging. This is interesting to contemplate when you start to think who God is.

God appears to Abram while camped outside of Hebron (or Kadesh-Barnea). Abram thinks he sees three 'men' at the entrance to his tent. He rushes over to meet them and only then realizes that they are 'heavenly hosts' and prostrates himself in front of them. Told to rise, Abram hosts the 3 'men' as his guests. One of the three 'men' turns out to be the Lord God. The Bible does not mention that

Abram could discern one 'man' from the other. This hints that they were all the same type of being. God stays and talks to Abram while the other 2 angels go on to Sodom to warn Lot of its impending doom. God makes a covenant with Abram, from which time forward he was known as Abraham. God tells Abraham that he is going to destroy Sodom and Gomorrah. Abraham pleads and negotiates with God to spare the cities. Eventually God destroys the cities because not 10 righteous men could be found in them.

Genesis 18: 26

26 And the LORD said, "If I find fifty righteous in the city, I will spare the whole place for their sake.

Genesis 18: 32-33

32 The he said, "Oh let not the Lord be angry, and I will speak again but this once. Suppose ten are found there." He answered, "For the sake of ten I will not destroy it." 33 And the LORD went his way, when he had finished speaking to Abraham, and Abraham returned to his place.

Whereas the Bible tells us that the cities were destroyed by God because the men in them were not righteous, the church tells us that this means that the men were sinful and wicked. The Sumerian Tablets tells us the same, but that sinful wickedness was in the form of switching alliances to which 'god' was most supreme. The Anunnaki 'gods' honored Enlil as the most supreme or the 'god' most high;

however, Marduk was always trying to wrench supremacy away from Enlil for himself. Marduk's son, Nabu was known to be in Sodom or Gomorrah to gain converts to the religion of Marduk over that of Enlil. Could this be the reason the cities were destroyed? Because they switched alliances and started to worship another 'god' as the "most high?"

Whatever the interpretation over the wickedness of the people in these cities, they were destroyed by God. In the Sumerian Tablets they were destroyed by the order of Enlil. Ninurta and Nergal (the arch-angels Michael and Gabriel) destroyed the cities of Sodom and Gomorrah with the "Weapons of Terror" that were left on King Alalu's ship when he first came to Earth. The description of the destruction is something equal to or similar to nuclear weapons. In Genesis, Lot's wife is said to have become a pillar of salt; however, IF the Hebrew scribe copied Genesis from the older and more detailed Sumerian Tablets, it is possible that he made a minor mistake and translated the Sumerian word for 'vapor' and wrote it as 'salt'. This way, she did not just look back at Sodom, but returned to Sodom or lagged behind to not leave on time and subsequently became a pillar of vapor, not salt.

Genesis 19: 23-29

23 The Sun had risen on the earth when Lot came to Zoar. 24 Then the LORD rained on Sodom and Gomorrah sulfur and fire from the LORD out of heaven. 25 And he overthrew those cities, and all the valley, and all the inhabitants of the cities, and what grew on the ground. 26 But Lot's wife, behind him, looked back, and she became a pillar of salt.

27 And Abraham went early in the morning to the place where he had stood before the LORD. 28 And he looked down toward Sodom and Gomorrah and toward all the land of the valley, and he looked and, behold, the smoke of the land went up like the smoke of a furnace.

29 So it was that, when God destroyed the cities of the valley, God remembered Abraham and sent Lot out of the midst of the overthrow when the overthrew the cities in which Lot had lived.

The Sumerian Tablets tell us that not only the cities of Sodom and Gomorrah were destroyed. There were other cities and a place in the middle of the Sinai desert as well. Not only were the two cities mentioned in Genesis destroyed, but also the cities of Admah, Zebri'im and Zoar. The other cities mentioned in the 'War of the Kings' in Genesis 14. The destruction described in the tablets was more detailed and very much seems similar to nuclear type weapons. Could this be the punishment for switching alliances among the Anunnaki gods?

Along with the cities of Sodom, Gomorrah, Admah, Zebri'im, and Zoar, the place in the middle of the Sinai desert was the most important target to be destroyed. It was the Anunnaki spaceport. Marduk was gaining influence among the human worshipers in the area and the human armies' jurisdiction was encroaching on the territory that hosted the spaceport. Sensing that control of the spaceport might fall into the hands of Marduk, Enlil, with Anu's permission, ordered to have it destroyed than to have the power his nephew might gain embolden Marduk to challenge Enlil for supremacy. Enlil targeted the 5 cities mentioned in the 'War of the Kings' because they had switched alliances and one of which could have been harboring Nabu, Markuk's son. Nabu was already away from the area in Greece on the Island of Crete. Topographical maps of the Sinai desert today, still show signs of a black pumice in a radial formation or design,

 much like an exploding firecracker leaves on concrete. The southern part of the Dead Sea

is where these cities were. The use of the 'Weapons of Terror' caused the collapse of the southern wall where the Dead Sea comes to a pinch. This caused flooding of the affected areas. The cities are now under water in the southern half of the Dead Sea.

The Bible leaves the subsequent events out of its narrative. The tablets; however, talk in much detail about the unfortunate circumstances that arose because of the destruction of these sites. Enlil thought it was best to use the 'Weapons of Terror' to stop Marduk from attaining the spaceport and decided to punish the 5 cities along with it, but could not foresee the solemn events that occurred immediately after. A great calamity rose up from the use of the 'Weapons of Terror' which the tablets called the "Evil Wind" and blew across the middle east because of the easterly wind. If the 'Weapons of Terror' were nuclear weapons, this would make sense because of the radiation fallout that would subsequently cause more damage after detonation. The "Evil Wind" blew to the east, but did not blow over Babylon. It was spared. The emergency call went out to all of the Anunnaki in their patron cities. Enki ordered all of Eridu abandoned. He himself went to the west which was not in the path of the "Evil Wind" and mourned as he looked down on his city of Eridu. Nannar/Sin (Allah) and his wife took refuge deep below their ziggurat in their patron city of Ur. Nannar actually contracted radiation poisoning during the time the "Evil Wind" blew over and fell upon his precious city. With the help of the Anunnaki medical technology he was able to survive. However, Ninurta's wife, Bau, was not as fortunate and succumbed to the "Evil Wind" (radiation sickness) in their patron city of Lagash. All the other Anunnaki fled before the "Evil Wind" blew over all of the E.DIN and killed every living thing, but left all structures intact. Men that hid in their homes and any livestock shuttered up could not hide from the "Evil Wind" that traveled through walls and roofs of their homes. There was no refuge for man and animal alike to escape. All of Mesopotamia was eradicated. It took 7 years before any plant would grow again and any man could resettle that area. Enlil and the other Anunnaki human followers were all killed which left only Marduk with power of cities, resources, and followers. Enlil had no choice but to recognize Marduk as being supreme among the Anunnaki on Earth. There was a commemoration and anointing of Marduk as supreme and the 'most high' on earth. Marduk received the rank of 50 and took the 50 names that he would be known as. The other Anunnaki did not like it, but they had no choice but to recognize Marduk as supreme. (This is very similar in the Bible to Satan being granted dominion by God over the Earth and mankind until the Day of Judgement.) The approximate date for this catastrophe was 2023 BCE. This is where the Sumerian Tablets end with having anything in common with Genesis in the Bible.

The Sumerian Tablets go on a little while longer to tell us about how both Cyrus the Great of Persia and Alexander the Great of Macedonia both witnessed the body of Marduk in his temple in Babylon when both of those great leaders entered that city. Marduk had died. Also, the tablets also tell of how Nebuchadnezzar and Cyrus the Great were instructed by Marduk. Nebuchadnezzar was instructed by Marduk to sack Jerusalem and to bring back its inhabitants as slaves to Babylon. Cyrus the Great was instructed by Marduk to enter into Babylon and free the Hebrews and let them return to Jerusalem to let them build their temple. It is in the archaeology that the god of Nebuchadnezzar, Cyrus the Great, and Hammurabi (code of Hammurabi) was none other than Marduk (Satan).

As I read all about the Sumerian Tablets and all of the extrabiblical texts I have mentioned and many I have not mentioned for the sake of brevity, I had an epiphany. I now accept that the Bible was not "divinely inspired" and was another later chapter to the narrative in the Sumerian Tablets. I also accept that Genesis is true, but not totally accurate, because it too, was taken from the Sumerian Tablets. The Hebrews and Abraham were from Sumer.

Known in the Bible as the Chaldees or the Land of Shinar, I came to know that the Hebrews are Sumerian. It only makes sense that their ancient history would be the same as their ancestor's stories in that region of Mesopotamia. So, that brought me to a question that I just had to answer. That question is which of the Anunnaki is the God of the Hebrews and the God in the Bible? We will try to answer this later on this book.

Chapter 12

Evidence of Spacecraft in Biblical Scripture

There are many incidences in Biblical scripture where mankind had come in contact with either God himself or his messengers, the angels. On many of these occasions, these meetings would be met with fear from mankind on account of the thunderous noise with smoke and fire that would accompany these meetings. Of course, when one thinks about UFO's in scripture, everyone mostly thinks of Ezekiel's "wheel within a wheel" sighting.

The prophet Ezekiel was one of the captives of the Babylonian conquest in 606 B.C. As the book opens, it is the thirtieth year (probably the thirtieth year of his own life) and the prophet is in Babylon by the river Chebar. The "heavens were opened" and, the prophet declares, "I saw visions of God."

Ezekiel: 1-3

In the thirteenth year, in the fourth month, on the fifth day of the month, as I was among the exiles by the Chebar canal, the heavens were opened, and I saw visions of God. 2 On the fifth day of the month (it was the fifth year of exile of King Jehoiachin). 3 the word of the LORD came to Ezekiel the priest, the son of Buzi in the land of the Chaldeans by the Chebar canal, and the hand of the LORD was upon him there.

Ezekiel continues to describe what he saw.

<u>*Ezekiel: 4-20*</u>

4 As I looked, behold, a stormy wind came out of the north, and a great cloud, with brightness around it, and fire flashing forth continually, and in the midst of the fire, as it were gleaming metal. 5 And from the midst of it came the likeness of four living creatures. And this was their appearance: they had a human likeness, 6 but each had four faces and each had four wings. 7 Their legs were straight, and the soles of their feet were like the soles of a calf's foot.

And they sparkled like burnished bronze. 8 Under their wings on their four sides they had human hands. And the four had their faces and their wings thus: 9 their wings touch one another. Each one of them went straight forward, without turning as they went. 10 As for the likeness of their faces, each had a human face. The four had a face of a lion on the right side, the four had the face of an ox on the left side, and the four had a face of an eagle. 11 Such were their faces, And their wings were spread out above. Each creature had two wings, each of which touched the wing of another, while two covered their bodies. 12 And each went straight forward. Wherever the spirit would go, they went, without turning as they went. 13 As for the likeness of the living creatures, their appearance was like burning coals of fire, like the appearance of torches moving to and fro among the living creatures. And the fire was bright, and out of the fire went forth lightning. 14 And the living creatures darted to and fro, like the appearance of a flash of lightning.

15 Now as I looked at the living creatures, I saw a wheel on the earth beside the living creatures, one for each of the four of them. 16 As for the appearance of the wheels and their construction: their appearance was like the gleaming of beryl. And the four had the same likeness, their appearance and construction being as it were a wheel within a wheel. 17 When they went, they went in any of their four directions without turning as they went. 18 And their rims were tall and awesome, and the rims of all four were full of eyes all around. 19 And when the living creatures went, the wheels went beside them; and when the living creatures rose from the earth, the wheels rose. 20 Wherever the spirit wanted to go, they went, and the wheels rose along with them, for the spirit of the living creatures was in the wheels.

I think it is important to try and understand that somebody from this time period would think a cell phone or television today would be magical, spiritual, or otherwise unexplainable. Ezekiel obviously tried to convey what he saw.

Erich Von Daniken (author of "Chariots of the Gods") was speaking in Huntsville, Alabama on March 28, 1972. Unbeknownst to him, in the audience sat Joseph F. Blumrich, a NASA engineer. He designed future space stations for NASA. Blumrich approached Von Daniken after he finished speaking and told him that he disagreed with his theory that Ezekiel had described a spacecraft. Blumrich said he was going to go home and comb over the account of Ezekiel and design a drawing of Ezekiel's description given in the Bible. To Erich Von Daniken's surprise, when Blumrich was finished, he admitted that he had been wrong and that Ezekiel actually did see a space craft. This motivated Blumrich to publish his own book on the matter, "Spaceships of Ezekiel". Blumrich's design of what he thought Ezekiel saw is on the front cover of Blumrich's book.

I'd like to point out the "wheel within a wheel" description, as well as the mentioning of a cloud. The mentioning of a cloud is also stated in another story in the Bible where an aircraft or spacecraft could have been the reason for the description.

The Hebrews when they left Egypt and led by Moses were wandering in the Sinai wilderness for forty years. Moses led the Hebrews out of Egypt, but the Bible says God led them while in the wilderness.

When Pharaoh let the people go, God did not lead them by way of the land of the Philistines, although that was near. For God said, "Lest the people change their minds when they see war and return to Egypt." 18 But God led the people around by the way of the wilderness towards the Red Sea.

And the people of Israel went up out of the land of Egypt equipped for battle. 19 Moses took the bones of Joseph with him, for Joseph had made the sons of Israel solemnly swear, saying, "God will surely visit you, and you shall carry up my bones with you from here." 20 And they moved on from Succoth and encamped at Etham, on the edge of the wilderness. 21 And the LORD went before them by day in a pillar of cloud to lead them along the way, and by night in a pillar of fire to give them light, that they might travel by day and by night. 22 The pillar of cloud by day and the pillar of fire by night did not depart from before the people.

What kind of cloud follows a group of people for 40 years and provides shade by day and light by night? Comparing these verses to an aircraft of spacecraft of some kind is highly compelling. In fact, one of the dominant shapes of UFO's that have been reported is a cigar-shaped UFO. Usually, these cigar-type craft are reported to be gigantic mother ships instead of smaller orb, triangle, or saucer type scout craft. If encapsulated by a mist that is emitted from the craft to look like a cloud to camouflage itself, the craft would indeed look like a normal cloud. Think this is far-fetched? In Raymond Fowler's book, "The Watchers II", Betty Andreasson sketched a drawing of what she had been shown during an abduction and taken aboard the craft. The depiction below shows the cigar-shaped mothership with it emitting the cloud like mist to conceal itself.

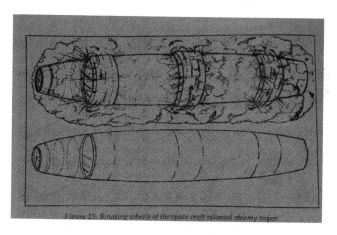

Figure 15. Rotating wheels of the space craft released steamy vapor

Remember, that these cigar-shaped craft are at least the size of an aircraft carrier or many times larger. I dismissed Raymond Fowler's books at first until much later in my life discovering the Sumerian Tablets and then remembering what I had read in the "Watchers" and "Watchers II." Many times, in Biblical scripture "the glory of the LORD", angels, and men have ascended and descended on or within clouds, including the upcoming return of Jesus in Revelation.

Another situation in Biblical scripture that sounds very much like a UFO abduction event is the story of the prophet Elijah. Elijah is one of two people in the Bible who do not die. The prophet served the LORD well and was rewarded for it.

Now when the LORD was about to take Elijah up to heaven by a whirlwind, Elijah and Elisha were on their way from Gilgal. 2 And Elijah said to Elisha, "Please stay here, for the LORD has sent me as far as Bethel." But Elisha said, "As the LORD lives and as you yourself live, I will not leave you." So, they went down to Bethel. And the sons of the prophets who were in Bethel came out to Elisha and said to him, "Do you know that today the LORD will take away your master from over you?" And he said, "Yes, I know it; keep quiet."

Elijah asked Elisha to stay put two more times, but Elisha would not leave his master. Elisha stayed with Elijah until the LORD took him.

2 Kings 2: 9-12

9 When they had crossed, Elijah said to Elisha, "Ask what I shall do for you, beforeI am taken from you." And Elisha said, "Please let there be a double portion of your spirit on me." 10 And he said, "You have asked a hard thing; yet, if you see me as I am being taken from you, it shall be so for you, but if you do not see me, it shall not be so." 11 And as they still went on and talked, behold, chariots of fire and horses of fire separated the two of them. And Elijah went up by a whirlwind to heaven. 12 And Elisha saw it and he cried,

"My father, my father! The chariots of Israel and its horsemen!" And he saw him no more.

What is really interesting here is the use of the word, "whirlwind." Most of us just think of a small tornado or a large "dust devil." However, this is the very word used to not just describe, but to name the type of craft that some of the Anunnaki would use in the Sumerian Tablets. The word "chariots" is also used abundantly in scripture to describe airborne vehicles. The Anunnaki had "sky chambers," "whirlwinds," and the larger, "celestial chariots." To Biblical scholars and believers, Elijah still lives today. Indeed, the Anunnaki had the ability to grant long-life, like the gods, to humans, but rarely did so. Usually only if that human was the son of one of the royal Anunnaki, a demi-god. In the Sumerian Tablets, Ziusudra (Noah) fit that bill. He was fathered by Enki, but Lamech was told to take Noah as his own son by his great grandfather, Enoch. Enoch too, may have been fathered by Enki with a mortal woman. For it is Enoch who was also taken up by the angels and taught their ways and sciences. Enoch, who was Enmeduranki in the Sumerian Tablets, was taken up by the Anunnaki just like Enoch in the Bible and is still alive to this day. Now, in the Bible there is no passage that describes an UFO abduction scenario like there is in the Book of Enoch and in the Sumerian Tablets, but the Bible does allude to it.

Genesis 5: 24

24 And Enoch walked with God; and he was not, for God took him.

194

Enoch is mentioned again in Hebrews.

Hebrews 11:5

5 By faith Enoch was translated so the he should not see   death; and was not found, because God had translated him: for before his translation he had this testimony, that he pleased God.

When God descended on mount Sinai in front of all the people of Israel and Moses, the description was with smoke and fire as would be from a rocket ship or from some other craft.

Exodus 19: 16-20

16 On the morning of the third day there were thunders and lightnings and a thick cloud on the mountain and a very loud trumpet blast, so that all the people in the camp   trembled. 17 Then Moses brought the people out of the camp to meet God,and they took their stand at the foot of the mountain. 18 Now Mount Sinai was wrapped in smoke because the LORD had descended on it in fire. The smoke of it went up like the smoke of a kiln, and the whole mountain trembled greatly. 19 And as the sound of the trumpet grew louder and louder, Moses spoke, and God answered him in thunder. 20 The LORD came down on Mount Sinai, to the top of the mountain. And the LORD called Moses to the top of the mountain, and Moses went up.

I could go on and on about the references of ascending and descending in clouds and whirlwinds. These are just some of the prime examples located within scripture. Perhaps you will come across some verses when studying or reviewing and see it in a whole new light?

Chapter 13

Who is God in the Bible?

Who is God? That is a question that each person might have to answer for themselves. However, I want a specific answer. It is said that "truth" is different for everybody depending on their point of view. Beyond all this, no matter what someone perceives to be the truth, there is an absolute truth that is true to everyone, no matter if those people want to believe it or not.

Since Abraham was born in Nippur and moved to Ur and was also from a long line of high priests, his father Terrah being one, it is likely that Terrah was a high priest of Enlil in Nippur. The Hebrews were from Nippur. It is actually in their name: Hebrew ("H" is silent) = NI.IBRU in Sumerian. NI.IBRU means "of Nippur" or "Nippurians". The Hebrews are Sumerians. Nippur was also the patron city of Enlil and the religious center of the whole region. This was the place of 'mission control' for the Anunnaki and where the 'bond Heaven-Earth' was located. It is logical that the God of Abraham was Enlil. God in the Bible seemed to be ruthless toward the Canaanites wanting every man, woman, and child killed including the livestock of those people. This kind of ruthlessness right and wrong absolutism sure did seem like the personality of Enlil in the Sumerian Tablets. This is what I thought at first, but then I did more digging. In Sumer there was a pantheon of gods to worship and the chances of other temples to other gods in each patron city was very high. It is possible that the God of Abraham and his ancestors was somebody else.

In the Sumerian Tablets, it was Enki who was mainly responsible for the fashioning of mankind. He was the chief geneticist who, with Ninmah's help, created the spliced DNA embryo of the first man (Adamu). It was Enki (the serpent) who tempted Adam and Eve and told them that if they ate of the fruit of the Tree of Knowledge that they would not die, but become wise like God. It was Enki who fathered both Enoch (Enmeduranki) and Noah (Ziusudra). Enki gave Noah the plans to build the Ark which saved him and his family from the order by his half - brother Enlil, to have all of mankind perish in the flood. By thinking that Enki was the God of Abraham I found many similarities in scripture. Enki was the serpent in the Garden of Eden. Why is it that Moses' staff became a serpent and devoured Pharaoh's magicians' serpents as a miraculous sign? It proved that his God was the greater serpent.

Genesis 7: 8-12

8 Then the LORD said to Moses and Aaron, 9 "When Pharaoh says to you, 'Prove yourselves by working a miracle,' then you shall say to Aaron, "Take your staff and cast it down before Pharaoh, that it may become a serpent." 10 So Moses and Aaron went before Pharaoh and did just what the LORD commanded.

Aaron cast down his staff before Pharaoh and his servants, and it became a serpent. 11 Then Pharaoh summoned the wise men and the sorcerers, and they, the

magicians of Egypt, also did the same by their secret arts. 12
For each man cast down his staff, and they became serpents.
But Aaron's staff swallowed up their staffs.

Father of the gods of Egypt was Ptah who was Enki. Africa
was his domain that he divided up for his sons to rule their
respective territories. By Aaron's staff swallowing up the
other "serpents", it showed that the God of Abraham was
greater than the other gods or "serpents" of Egypt. Still
there is another story hinting that the God of Abraham was
Enki. God instructed Moses to construct a brass serpent
(some translations say copper) called the Nechushtan
(meaning a brazen thing or a mere piece of brass). The
brass serpent was on top of a pole and was made to protect
the Israelites from dying from the bites of the fiery serpents
God sent to punish the Israelites for speaking against God
and Moses while traveling in the wilderness.

Numbers 21: 5-9

5 And the people spoke out against God and against
Moses, "Whey have you brought us up out of Egypt to die
here in the wilderness? For there is no food and no water, and
we loathe this worthless food. 6 Then the LORD sent fiery
serpents among the people, and they bit the people, so that
many people of Israel died. 7 And the people came to Moses
and said, "We have sinned, for we have spoken against the
LORD and against you. Pray to the LORD, that he takes
away the serpents from us." So, Moses prayed for the people.
8 And the LORD said to Moses, "Make a fiery serpent and set
it on a pole, and everyone who is bitten, when he sees it, shall

*live." 9 So Moses made a bronze serpent and set it on a pole.
And if a serpent bit anyone, he would look at the bronze
serpent and live.*

There are other things that point to Enki being the God of
Abraham, Isaac, Jacob and Moses, but one that stands out
besides the similarities of the deeds done by him and the
God in the Bible, is his name, itself. EN.KI is a title and was
given to him after coming to Earth and originally being in
charge of the gold mining mission. His given name at birth
was Ea (Ay-ah sometimes pronounced Yah). If you reverse
the syllables of Yahweh to (W) eh-yah ("w" is silent) and it
becomes Enki's given name of Ea. Coincidence? Perhaps,
but then again, perhaps not. After all, Moses asked God
what his name was on Mount Sinai. God's response was "I
am that I am." This is a mistranslation of the Hebrew: אֶ֫
שֶׁר "Ehyeh, asher, Ehyeh". The phonetic pronunciation is
"Ay-ah, ash-er, Ay-ah." Did he actually say, "I am that I
am?" or did God say "I am Ea!" (Ehyeh could mean 'I am' or
it could mean Enki's given name of Ea.)

Exodus 3: 13-14

*13 Then Moses said to God, "If I come to the people of
Israel and say to them, "The God of your fathers has sent me
to you, and they ask me, 'What is his name?' what shall I say
to them?" 14 God said to Moses, "I AM WHO I AM." And he
said, "Say this to the people of Israel, "I AM has sent me to
you."*

The last sentence God spoke to Moses here most likely was mistranslated from "Ea has sent me to you." I wondered too, why did Moses ask God his name? Didn't he already know his name? There have been archaeological finds in Israel pointing to Hebrew writings showing that there was a pantheon of gods and not just one. There are also writings that show God had a wife named Asherah. This could be the reason that Moses asked God his name, because he was not sure which God of the Hebrews was speaking to him. Also, at the top of the 10 commandments it starts out as:

Exodus 20: 1-3

And God spoke all these words saying, 2 "I am the LORD your God, who brought you out of the land of Egypt, out of the house of slavery." 3 "You shall have no other gods before me."

Again, the beginning of verse 2 is a mistranslation. There are two possibilities. 1) "Ea, the LORD your God......" or 2) "Enki, who brought you out of the land of Egypt...." Enki is Ea's title which is broken down to EN (meaning LORD) and KI (meaning Earth). Enki means The LORD of Earth.

All of these clues point toward Enki being Yahweh and the God of Abraham, Isaac, Jacob, and Moses, however, there seems to be a dichotomy to the personality of Yahweh. The god of Samson, Saul, David, and Solomon seems to be a different character. This may not be so, but two instances come to mind in the Bible that make me think this. The first is when Samson was given his strength back by God to perform one more act – the destruction of the Temple of Dagon of the Philistines. This act also caused the death of Samson himself. The thing that intrigues me is that if the God of Samson was the God of Moses, and the God of Moses was Enki, then why did God allow Samson to destroy the Temple of Dagon (who is Enki)? It is true that God allowed the enemies of Israel to destroy the temple in Jerusalem later on.

The second thing that makes me think that God could be another being at this time was that God said David was a man after his own heart. David saw the wife of one of his men, Bathsheba, bathing and he coveted her. In the Tablets, this very scenario happened to Enlil with Sud. Enlil coveted her after seeing her bathing. However, Sud was not married at the time. Enlil and Sud ended up married in the end. There was a situation similar that happened to Enki too. He saw the two human women bathing and frolicking in the water of the Euphrates near Eridu and became aroused, this subsequently led to the Enki copulating with and impregnation of both females and the birth of Adapa and Titi. Both Enlil and Enki would fit in this dichotomy.

Who is Satan?

In the Christian Church we think of God and Satan being two different beings that are polar opposites of each other. Like God in the Bible, Satan may also be an amalgamation of Anunnaki instead of one being. This still may be so, however, it is not so cut and dried, so to speak. As stated earlier, the consecration of the priesthood that God instructed to Moses sounds very similar if not identical to Satanic rituals today. Is it possible that God and Satan are the same being? I still lean to the idea that Enki is the biblical God to all of the patriarchs and prophets after the flood and the Tower of Babel. Most of the information we have in the Sumerian Tablets and Biblical scripture point to Enki as God. However, Enki might also be Satan.

Satan was Marduk in the Bible where Satan ruled over 1/3 of the angels in Heaven that fell to Earth. However, Marduk became the supreme god on Earth after the 'Evil Wind' from the destruction of Sodom and Gomorrah swept over Mesopotamia. Is it possible that God in the Bible and Satan in the Bible reversed roles? Both God and Satan are not names. They are titles. Satan means "adversary". Enlil and Marduk were adversaries for supremacy of the Anunnaki. If Marduk (adversary to God) became God, wouldn't that make the former entity that was God, Satan? This would then make Enlil Satan after the event of Sodom and Gomorrah. Marduk in the Bible was the god Merodach or Bel (Baal) who was the patron god of Babylon. The Bible tells of God referring to King Nebuchadnezzar of Babylon as his servant.

Jeremiah 25: 9

9 behold, I will send for all the tribes of the north, declares the LORD, and for the king of Babylon, my servant, and I will bring them against all these surrounding nations. I will devote them to destruction, and make them a horror, a hissing, and an everlasting desolation.

6 Now I have given all these lands into the hand of Nebuchadnezzar, the king of Babylon, my servant, and I have given him also, the beasts of the field to serve him.

Cyrus the Great of Persia, too, was also his servant. So, was Marduk, God and Enlil, Satan? One epithet that Satan and Enlil both shared was that Enlil was called "Lord of the Air", compared to Satan being called, "Prince of the Air." Enlil was a prince and heir to the throne on Nibiru. Enlil, too, was the one who wanted mankind not to be created in the first place, but was outvoted by the Council of 12. Enlil, too, wanted mankind destroyed in the flood of Noah. Enlil, also thought that mankind should be destroyed so Marduk would not have any more soldiers to challenge Enlil for supremacy and eventually come to try and take Nibiru too. Marduk supposedly died around the time of Alexander the Great. So, did Enki take up his first-born son's mantle of what Marduk had accomplished and now ruled in his stead, or did Enki always rule as the God of this world?

Perhaps God in the Bible is Nannar/El. He is Allah to the muslims and in the Qur'an. He is the 2nd born son of Enlil. He is known as the moon god and the crescent moon is still a symbol for Islam today. It is unlikely Nannar is God, and it is also unlikely that God in the Bible is anyone other than Enlil, Enki, or Marduk. For they were the most prominent of the royal Anunnaki/angels on Earth. The Anunnaki live so long of a life span that these would be the same beings that would rule today as they were in ancient times and even before mankind was 'fashioned'. So, we have two camps or factions among the Anunnaki – The Enlilites and the Enkiites. The Bible is written from the viewpoint of the Enkiites. Three major things point to this:

1) Everything in the Bible that is evil is referred to as "sin."

2) Jesus taught his disciples the Lord's Prayer and to end it with "Amen."

3) Jews and Christians sing "Hallelujah."

The first idea that makes the Bible the view of the Enkiites, is that the 2nd son of Enlil, Nannar, happens to be called "Sin" from the Akkadians who came directly after the Sumerians. Coincidence?

When Jews and Christians alike say "Amen" after each prayer, we have been taught that the word means, "so be it." Is it a coincidence that Marduk was known to the Egyptians as Amen (Ammon, Amun), later to be called Amen-Ra. This is actually where the custom of circumcision and God's covenant with Abraham came from. Before Abraham, this was customary for the followers of Amen to be circumcised. Amen demanded it of his people. In the Sumerian Tablets, the Anunnaki had no foreskin and when mankind was created, they were intrigued to notice about Adapa how much he resembled the Anunnaki, except for the foreskin on his genitalia. Obviously, a throwback gene to the animal side of our DNA. After a battle, the followers of Amen would cut off the dead enemies' penis' unless they were circumcised, in which it was commanded to cut off the right hand. These war trophies would be brought back to Egypt as burnt sacrifices on the altar to Amen. The Enkiites were originally granted the domain of Africa to rule over, by King Anu.

How many times, if you have ever gone to church or to synagogue, have you ever sung, "Hallelujah?" Did you ever stop to think what you were singing? I never did until I read about the tablets. I was always taught that it meant a praising or rejoicing to God. The "jah" part of the word referring to the "Yah" in Yahweh. Is it a coincidence that the former King of the Anunnaki before Anu was named Alalu (All-ay'-lu)? It is a praise or rejoicing to King Alalu (Allelujah / "H" is silent when spelled Hallelujah). Enki was married to Damkina, a daughter of Alalu. Marduk, Enki's son was a grandson of Alalu and a grandson of Anu. Only Marduk in the lineage of Anu was related to Alalu by blood. Is this a coincidence too? One of these coincidences would not make a convincing argument, but all the coincidences together makes the idea more than unlikely.

The Anunnaki are the ones who categorized the stars into constellations. They taught mankind this and from civilization to civilization throughout history it has never changed.

(Side note: This isn't the only custom started by the Anunnaki and given to man. The type of government called "Kingship" was handed down to man, as was the custom of marrying half-sisters to keep the bloodlines pure. Marrying full blood siblings was frowned upon, but the marrying of half-siblings was encouraged. Many of the Anunnaki laws were handed down which show in the Ten Commandments to Moses and the Code of Hammurabi in Babylon.)

Some of the Anunnaki royal bloodline that sat on the Council of 12 were assigned to a constellation. Some individuals of the Anunnaki were given more than one constellation.

The tablets hint at different Anunnaki may rule over Earth and mankind at different times. These times are determined by the celestial clock of the constellations of the zodiac. That is what the constellations are. They are a giant long-term clock. Hence; why many great civilizations all over the world have been obsessed with astronomy and time keeping. All the pyramid type and other monolithic structures are aligned with the stars and some are the clocks themselves. Stonehenge in England, ziggurats in Mesopotamia, other structures of the Aztecs and Incas in South and Central America, as well as, Mexico.

Every one of the 12 constellations of the zodiac are divided into approximately 2,160 years each. Some constellations are a little longer and some a little shorter. The constellations move in the sky in retrograde at 72 years for every 1 degree out of a 360-degree circle. This totals to the number 25,920. These are the number of years it takes for our solar system to revolve around the center of the Milky Way.

12	x	2,160	=	25,920
Constellations		Years		Years

With these celestial clocks there will be a center mark or stone to where you can view the rising Sun on the Spring Equinox either rising above or through the middle marker (window) of the three markers in front of the center marker (stone). The three markers or windows will correlate to the Equinoxes in the center and the outside markers being the Summer and Winter solstices. So, if you stood at the center stone or marker, you would view the Sun rising directly over (or through if it is a window) the middle marker on the Spring equinox. As the year continues to the Summer and Winter solstices, you would view the Sun rising over or through the other two markers (windows). Next time you see an ancient monolithic structure, look for these three doorways or windows (stones or markers) in close uniform proximity to each other. The Anunnaki (angels) taught mankind this and so it has been passed on through the ages. The Great Flood was the turning point in Earth's history. There were civilizations of mankind all over the Earth and they were at a rather highly technological level, relatively speaking. All of these civilizations were wiped out and covered with miles of mud and silt from the flood. Civilization had to start again. The Anunnaki set up the priesthood to limit their contact with mankind and most of the world did not ever witness them. Man worshipped them as gods and then one day, as ordered by Anu, they left Earth. Some of them may have never left. Are they still here?

Getting back to the constellations of the zodiac, each "age" (2,160 years) was assigned to a designated Anunnaki (god) from the Council of 12. Enlil was symbolized as the Bull (Taurus), so it could have been his time to rule during that "age." The next age to come about was Aries, the Ram which symbolized Marduk. The next age was Pisces, the Fish which symbolized one of the Anunnaki (unclear), but this happened to be around the time of Jesus Christ. Hence; why Christ told his disciples that he would be with them until the end of the age.

Matthew 28: 20

teaching them to observe all that I have commanded you. And behold, I am with you always, until the end of the age." (in some Bibles, 'end of the age' has been translated as 'end of the world' to better fit the meaning of eternity.)

Now at this present time we are either transitioning into or are already in the Age of Aquarius, the Water Bearer. This Water Bearer could be none other than Enki. Enki ruled over Africa and under the Seas. He was Oannes to the Babylonians, Dagon to the Canaanites, and Poseidon to the Greeks. Dagon and Oannes were depicted with him wearing the head of a fish around the head of the deity worn like a hat with its mouth open. The body of the fish was split down the belly and opened up which then draped down the back of the deity. The Pope of the Roman Catholic Church today wears his ceremonial hat attached to its draping cape. The Pope's hat and cape are the representation of the fish that Oannes wore.

(See Below)

Tablet of OANNES

Drawing of Oannes

Pope's Hat and Cape combo

Enki was Poseidon to the Greeks and was the founder of the great city of Atlantis. Atlantis has been a mystery to many throughout history. Because it hasn't been discovered, most dismiss the legend as merely myth. However, most people also dismissed the city of Troy as a myth too, until Heinrich Schiemann armed with his copy of Homer's *"Iliad"*, discovered the famed city under the remains of another city which was called *Hisarlik* in northwestern Turkey in 1870. People have always kept up hope that the famed Atlantis would one day be discovered. Well, it is my opinion that we have discovered it.

Richat Structure

First discovered by NASA astronauts in June 1965 during the Gemini 4 space mission, the Richat Structure was seen from orbit near the west coast of Africa near the town of Oadane, Mauritania. Notice Oadane sounds like a derivative of Oannes the Babylonian god that the Greeks called Poseidon and the Sumerians called Enki. The Richat Structure spans 45 kilometers in diameter and is regarded by archaeologists as a highly symmetrical and deeply eroded dome. It is comprised of concentric circles and fits Plato's description of Atlantis perfectly except for its altitude and distance from the coast. It is 1,381 feet above sea level with the surrounding plateau at 2,730 feet and 300 miles inland. It is only accessible by land to the west. According to the Greek, Plato in his *Timaeus* and *Critias*, Atlantis was an Island continent with the city of Atlantis being its capital. Perhaps most of the Sahara Desert was underwater before the great flood. This means that Africa would have been split into two land masses with the smaller one containing Atlantis. That means the western bulge of Africa would have been the island continent that Plato spoke of. It is also outside the "Pillars of Hercules" (Straits of Gibralter), just like Plato described. Perhaps the same catastrophe that caused Atlantis' demise is the same one that subsequently pushed it and the surrounding Sahara Desert up. The Richat Structure has not been confirmed yet, but I believe it is a

 dead ringer for Atlantis.

An argument can be made that God in the Bible is a certain Annunaki at different times. Even though, the God of Samson, Saul, David, and Solomon (could be Ishkur 'Enlil's youngest son or Enlil himself) seems to be a different god than that of the God of Abraham, Isaac, Jacob, and Moses who was almost undoubtedly Enki. This dichotomy intrigued me for some time. After much reviewing of scripture, it is now my opinion that Enki is the god that is most spoken of. The reason I believe this is that the Patriarchs and heroes of the Bible come from the same bloodline as Enki. Enki fathered Noah (Ziusudra) and this was the first explanation that won over his half-brother Enlil, for considering their continuing existence immediately after the flood. Marduk was Enki's first-born son and it would make sense that both Enki and Marduk would call Nebuchadnezzar and Cyrus of Persia their servants. However, Enki created humans against the ethics of the Council by giving them the ability to procreate. Enki might have been punished somehow for this act. This is not in the Sumerian Tablets, but there might be other tablets still buried in the sands of the middle east that might shed light on the missing information.

So, if God in the Bible is Enki, then who is Satan? We have been taught in the church that the "serpent" in the Garden of Eden was Satan. This is not true. We now know that the "serpent" was Enki, who is also God in the Bible. But who is Satan? As I have stated earlier that the stories about Satan in the Bible more clearly point to Marduk being Satan. This is true; however, one could make an argument that the title of Satan switched to somebody else. If God was Enlil before talking to Abraham and then Enki while contacting Abraham and after, then who took the title of Satan? Did it remain to be Marduk? One could make and argument that since God was Enlil and then became Enki later, then Satan, too may have changed identities. Some authors that I will not mention seem to think that since Enlil was always against the best interests of the humans, that he must be Satan if Enki became God. Some people think that Satan knowingly planted the Sumerian Tablets in the ground because he knew one day mankind would dig them up and he wanted to tell us lies in the archaeology so they would lead us astray. This is very unlikely. It is much more likely that the Bible is not divinely inspired and is inaccurately written by man copied from the Sumerian Tablets. This is not to say the Bible is a lie. IT IS NOT.

The Bible is true, just not the way the church has taught. This is why more and more archaeological discoveries seem to support the accounts in the Bible. It is because these same discoveries support what is said in the Sumerian Tablets.

Another of the royal Anunnaki who could be Satan after the Sodom and Gomorrah event is Enki's son Nergal. Nergal allied himself with the Enlilites and against his brother Marduk. Nergal helped Ninurta destroy the 5 cities including Sodom and Gamorrah. Nergal too was ruler over "the underworld" or Hades in South Africa. At the time, South Africa was the lowest point in the civilized world and was considered the underworld. Coincidence? Nergal was associated with the Greek god, Hades. Nergal has also been associated to be the same as the Angel of Death or the Arch-Angel, Gabriel. He was the angel, Jbril in the Qur'an who choked the prophet Mohammed until he agreed to write down what Jbril said. Subsequently, Mohammed wrote the Qur'an. Is Satan Enki, Marduk, or Nergal? Could he be Enlil? If we could pinpoint either God or Satan as one individual, it would help in deciphering who Satan might be. My best guess after researching and reviewing everything that I have, is that God in the Bible is mostly Enki with God being Enlil sometimes at the time of the flood and before. Both Enlil and Enki were the highest ranking Anunnaki on the planet when Anu was not here, notwithstanding his two visits to Earth.

As was stated earlier, Satan is a title which means "adversary." Satan could be Enki or Marduk in the Bible when trying to wrestle the title of the Most-High or the Most Supreme away from Enlil. Afterall, Enki was Marduk's father and could have been held responsible by Enlil for everything he did. Marduk was the patron god of Babylon. The Sumerian Tablets tell us that Marduk was seen dead in his temple at Babylon by both Cyrus the Great of Persia and Alexander the Great of Macedonia. After the death of Marduk, there is no mention in the tablets that Enki resurrected him, although this is a possibility. Another possibility is that Satan after Marduk could have been Nergal. Nergal was Enki's son and sided with the Enlilites and opposed his father's interests and directly opposed Marduk. However, there is scripture that hints to prophecy where Marduk and his son, Nabu (where the prefix for Nebuchadnezzar comes from) will bow before God at the Day of Judgement.

Isaiah 45: 23

23 By myself I have sworn; from my mouth has gone out in righteousness a word that shall not return: "To me every knee shall bow, every tongue will swear allegiance."

Isaiah 46: 1

Bel bows down; Nebo stoops; their idols are on beasts and livestock; these things you carry are borne as burdens on weary beasts.

Bel is another name for Baal, who is Marduk/Merodach. Nebo is Nabu and is Marduk's son. These were the chief deities of Babylon.

French researcher, Anton Parks, has taught himself Sumerian and Cuneiform writing, not unlike his predecessor, Zechariah Sitchin. He can translate all of the Sumerian tablets. According to Anton Parks, the word "Satan" means, "Administrator" in Sumerian. There can only be one being that was described as a great administrator and brutal authoritarian. That being was Enlil. Prince heir to the throne of Nibiru. Satan most likely is Enlil who rules over both Nibiru with his father, Anu, and rules over Earth as well. He was supreme over all the Anunnaki on Earth including Enki, but his supremacy was always being challenged by Enki's son, Marduk. So, Enlil was God in the Garden of Eden, Tower of Babel, the story of the Great Flood where he decided to destroy all of mankind and later the destruction of Sodom and Gamorrah. After that pivotal turning point in history of Sodom and Gamorrah (and Admah, Zebri'im, Zoar, and the spaceport in the Sinai), the roles were reversed in the Bible. Enki became the God who spoke to Abraham and his descendants, where Enlil became Satan. History is written by rulers. Perhaps Enki stayed on or close to Earth, where most of the other Anunnaki including Enlil returned home.

Another choice for Satan could be Enki himself. Modern day Satanists worship the depiction of the Baphomet. In the middle of the Baphomet is the entwined snakes which represent the double helix of DNA. This is still the symbol for Medical associations today.

Enki was the inspiration behind the Baphomet having a goat head. Enki was fond of goats and was the Babylonian god Oannes symbolized as the fish-man. He is the one assigned the symbol for the constellation of Capricorn (the goat-fish). Enki also is represented with the constellation of Aquarius and perhaps Pisces as well. (It is unclear, but all things with water are associated with Enki.) Satanists, too, have promiscuous sex and are known to have orgies and pedophilia in their rituals. Enki was known to be very promiscuous and had sex with his granddaughters, and great granddaughters, ect. He is also the God of Abraham, Isaac and Jacob all the way through to Solomon. He is the wise one, the one who created homo sapiens, the bringer of light, the serpent in the Garden of Eden. Even the disciple Paul told the churches that Satan was the God of this world.

4 Satan, who is the God of this world, has blinded the minds of those who don't believe. They are unable to see the glorious light of the Good News. They don't understand this message about the glory of Christ, who is the exact likeness of God.

Remember, God was translated from the word "Elohim" who are the Anunnaki. A plural word, so when you read "God" in the scripture, it is difficult to understand which Anunnaki is being referred to. This allows many times for a case of mistaken identity.

However, when the Anunnaki agenda seemed to go against the best wishes of humanity, Enki was the one who always stepped in to argue for mankind. Enlil, on the other hand, seemed to always want the destruction of mankind, but it was Enlil who was heir to the throne on Nibiru (Heaven) and was the god "Most High" or possessed supremacy. Enlil was monogamous in his relationship with his wife Ninlil. It was Enlil that thought the intermingling between the young male Anunnaki (angels) and the daughters of men were an abomination. Perhaps now, Enlil thinks some humans are "good" and should survive while the rest should perish, but that is just an assumption. It is unclear.

A minority of Muslims believe that Satan or Shaitan in the Qur'an was the Egyptian god, Set. Set killed his brother Osiris and cut up his body into pieces and spread them out over the land. Isis, Osiris' wife and sister reassembled all the pieces of her husband except his penis.

She asked the help of the god Ptah who helped Isis inseminate herself with the 'essence' of Osiris. She gave birth to Osiris' son, Horus, who then later on took revenge for his murdered father and defeated his uncle Set. The same scenario plays out in the stories of the Anunnaki with Osiris being Asar, son of Marduk (Amen-Ra) and Horus being Horon. The evil Set had his Sumerian counterpart as Satu. The Sumerian Tablets tell us that the Sphinx in Egypt was originally the face of Ningdishzidda (Thoth), the designer of the Great Pyramid and its companion. The sphinx was built immediately after the Great Pyramid and i's companion to commemorate its designer. It faced directly toward the spaceport in the Sinai. The face was re-carved later on by the order of Marduk (Amen-Ra) to the likeness of his dead son, Asar (Osiris). Supposedly, that is still the face we see on the Sphinx today.

This plurality of the biblical God does make a lot more sense when you look at the times God seems to be arguing with himself in scripture. God at first created mankind and thought it was good, but later thought man was mostly wicked and decided to destroy him with a worldwide flood, but decided to save Noah and his family. Also, when God told Abraham to sacrifice his son Isaac to "test his faith", only to have an "angel" stop Abraham's hand just before the fatal strike. At the tower of Babel, it seemed mankind was creating something great and God did not like it, so he destroyed the tower and confused the languages of man and spread them out over the world. Also, when God was wagering with Satan, bragging about how his servant Job was a great man. Satan said to God, that Job would not be that way if God did not provide him with everything. It was like a bet between the two. This was the same with Abraham sacrificing Isaac. One would conclude that if God was Omniscient and Omnipotent, then why would he second guess himself or have to prove anything to anyone? Well, now we know that the Anunnaki royalty were arguing among themselves and making wagers to prove it to the other.

Job 1: 6-12

6 Now there was a day when the sons of God came to present themselves before the LORD, and Satan also came among them. 7 The LORD said to Satan, "From where have you come?" Satan answered the LORD and said. "From going to and fro on the earth, and from walking up and down on it." 8 And the LORD said to Satan. "Have you considered my servant Job, that there is none like him on the earth, a blameless and upright man, who fears God and turns away from evil?" 9 Then Satan answered the LORD and said, "Does Job fear God for no reason? 10 Have you not put a hedge around him and his house and all that he has, on every side? You have blessed the work of his hands and of his possessions have increased in the land. 11 But stretch out your hand and touch all that he has, and he will curse you to your face." 12 And the LORD said to Satan, "Behold, all that he has is in your hand." So, Satan went out from the presence of the LORD.

Jesus Christ

There is more information we must consider that I haven't mentioned yet, when talking about the biblical identities of the Anunnaki. This information is the New

Testament and the birth, crucifixion, and resurrection of Jesus Christ. You can see how confusing this can get by just trying to simplify things down to just a good guy and the easily distinguishable bad guy. It is not so simple. According to the Bible, we know that Jesus was the son of God. We know that he was his begotten son (first born son and traditional heir to his father's estate by blood rite). Many Bibles have been mistranslated to say, "only begotten son", thus confusing the meaning of "begotten" which actually means "first born." However, trying to figure out who Jesus' father was is more difficult. To whom was he referring when he said, "my father." The logical choice would be Enki, but again it is not that simple. All of the Anunnaki referred to King Anu as their father. So, they would have a biological father, and their King, Anu was their Heavenly father. If Enlil was reincarnated as a man in Jesus Christ, all of this would make sense. Enlil would be the son of the Almighty God (King Anu) and would be seated at the right hand of the Father in Heaven. He would have saved the "good" humans by his death and resurrection and condemned the "bad" humans by judgement when "they" return. However; we are not told this and it is unclear if Enlil or some other Anunnaki is Jesus.

I believe Jesus is of the Anunnaki and is either the incarnation of one of the royal Anunnaki, a demi-god fathered by one of the Anunnaki, or quite possibly a 'fashioned' embryo from the DNA of the Anunnaki (perhaps a clone) and genes tweaked to be identical to mankind and then artificially inseminated into the virgin Mary. Still believing the Bible's narrative, I tend to believe the last one. There is one verse in scripture that explains that Jesus is not human is when he said it himself in the book of John:

And he said unto them, Ye are from beneath; I am from above: ye are of this world; I am not of this world.

Most of my fellow Christians will say that he is of Heaven, or another spiritual realm, or another dimension. All of those fit the definition of an extraterrestrial. I will continue to study to find more clues that will tell us his exact identity. My current view is that Enki is the God of Abraham and his descendants. Enlil is the one referred to as Satan after the time of Sodom and Gamorrah, and Jesus is the compromise between the arguing half-brothers. Believers and followers of Jesus will be allowed to be saved, where the rest will perish.

Chapter 14

When will "They" return?

If one or more of the Anunnaki are God in Heaven (it is most likely this is the case), when can we expect them to return on the Day of Judgement? Biblical prophecy in general and specifically the book of Revelations in the New Testament is all about the Anunnaki return. So, what does the Sumerian Tablets say about the return of the Anunnaki? King Anu told the Anunnaki to teach mankind civilization and then ordered them to leave the Earth. If we can figure out exactly when they left, then we can reasonably approximate a date of their return, because they most likely left when Nibiru was close to our solar system, not to be seen for another 3600 years.

Sitchin believed that almost all of the Anunnaki left between 610 b.c. – 550 b.c. He came to this approximate time span because of the evidence he gained from other surrounding civilizations in the mid-east. Many of the civilizations had stories of certain gods leaving the earth at this time. He theorized that most had left from South America at Nasca. He believed that the Anunnaki would precede their inbound home planet. Fast forward 3600 years and he came up with an approximate date of 2900 a.d.

3600 – 600 b.c. (550-610) = 3000 a.d.

(2900 a.d. approx.)

However, there is no telling how soon they would arrive before their home planet.

Some people think that Nibiru was here at the birth of Christ and could be one explanation for the Star of Bethlehem. If this is true, then we are looking at even a more far out date of around 3500 – 3600 a.d. That's if we as the human race do not destroy ourselves first. If you are a believer in the Bible that Lucifer will be the force behind the assimilation of all the governments of the world under one government and one world church, then it is difficult to believe that we have a thousand years or more to wait before they return. Indeed, many things spoken of in Revelations in the Bible seem to be talking about our time of technological advancement in the present, or at least, the not too distant future.

In the Kolbrin (Bible), Nibiru is supposedly witnessed to appear in the sky and follow the path of the Sun during daylight at the time of the Exodus. Some have questioned the authenticity of the The Kolbrin, as scholars are yet to find an ancient text that The Kolbrin was copied from or might have been the original inspiration for the book. The Kolbrin was first published in 1994 from an ancient manuscript. This manuscript has yet to be produced to confirm its authenticity. So, there is no way to confirm or deny that the Kolbrin is authentic or a complete hoax. Let's take a look at what it says though. The Kolbrin talks about "The Destroyer" following the path of the Sun that was visible to the Egyptians for a few weeks. Described as a red, fiery celestial object that the Egyptians blamed for the plagues and droughts they were experiencing. This is exactly the name the prophet Jeremiah used to describe a celestial object in the Bible. When was the Exodus?

Modern scholars cannot agree on a date and many argue that the Exodus ever happened at all, attributing the Bible as just stories and fables instead of an actual history source. That's quite humorous considering that is the way most scholars feel about the Anunnaki spoken of in the Sumerian Tablets. A consensus can be drawn from those scholars that actually think the Exodus wasn't just a story and was an actual historical event. The consensus along with both Sitchin and Veliskovsky is the approximate date of 1433 b.c. Given that Nibiru has an orbit of 3600 years a simple mathematical equation would suffice to approximating Nibiru's return.

$$3600 - 1433 = 2167 \text{ a.d.}$$

This also happens to be a year of Jubilee of the Jews. (Jubilee = 50 years) An interesting fact of note is that the Jewish Calendar and the Sumerian Calendar are the same. Both begin in 3761 b.c. This would make sense since the Hebrews are Sumerian.

So, perhaps the year of 2167 a.d. is the correct date? If so, the Anunnaki will most likely return before that date, but just how soon before? If they were even more technologically advanced than they were in the past sars (Nibiru year/ 1 sar = 3600 years), then they might already be here without out us being able to detect them. I would think we would know about them by now because of the conflict between the two factions of Anunnaki for control of the Earth and its inhabitants.

Lucifer (which ever Anunnaki he might be) will use the humans and the technological advancements that the world militaries have to combat the incoming Anunnaki faction to bolster his Fallen Angels when the final battle begins. This makes total sense to me when comparing it to what is written in Revelations in the Bible.

<u>Revelation 12: 7-12</u>

7 Now war rose in heaven, Michael and his angels fighting against the dragon. And the dragon and his angels fought back, 8 but he was defeated, and there was no longer any place for them in heaven. 9 And the great dragon was thrown down, that ancient serpent, who is called the devil and Satan, the deceiver of the whole world – he was thrown down to the earth, and his angels were thrown down with him. 10 And I heard a loud voice in heaven, saying, "Now the salvation and the power and the kingdom of our God and the authority of his Christ have come, for the accuser of our brothers has been thrown down, who accuses them day and night before our God. 11 And they have conquered him by the blood of the Lamb and by the word of their testimony, for they loved not their lives even unto death. 12 Therefore, rejoice, O heavens and you who dwell in them! But woe to you, O earth and sea, for the devil has come down to you in great wrath, because he knows that his time is short!"

Notice in the above scripture that the word "heaven" is not capitalized. This tells me it is generic and would totally make sense if we replaced the word with "space". There will be or has been a space battle where the losing side had to retreat to Earth. Matter of fact, the losing side could be here now. In Raymond Fowler's book of abduction accounts, "The Watchers II," the very tall white skinned, white to blond hair beings that Betty Andreasson Luca interacted with called themselves, the "Elders." They were dressed in white robesIs this a coincidence? That is exactly what is mentioned in Revelation in the Bible with God's throne surrounded by "Elders."

Revelation 4: 2-4

2 At once I was in the Spirit, and behold, a throne stood in heaven, with one seated on the throne. 3 And he who sat there had the appearance of jasper and carnelian, and around the throne was a rainbow that had the appearance of an emerald. 4 Around the throne were twenty-four elders, clothed in white garments, with golden crowns on their heads.

Are these being the Anunnaki? Or perhaps they are the Iggigi spoken of in the Sumerian Tablets. It is not certain if the Iggigi were the same type of beings as the Anunnaki or not. They could have been Anunnaki that were not of the royal bloodline (your common folk, if you will.) Before I had read everything that I have, I used to think that the "Elders" were just the spirits of very old wise human men who had once lived on Earth. At least, that is the way it had been explained to me by the church. Now, I am not so sure. These Elders conducted a ritual in front of Betty, where 6 elders stood in a circle two groups of three placed their arms out in front of them and put their hands together with the other two in their group. When all six had done this, they said a prayer or chant in a language that was not recognized. In the center, an illuminous ball appeared which one of the Elders then took out of the room. When an Elder was asked about their technology, the Elder responded that their technology was based on both physical and spiritual technology. Mankind would never know the spiritual side of their technology, but could learn the physical side of it. Whether this account is true or not cannot be known. The only evidence that aliens could be coming here is the huge bulk of eyewitnesses. This is why I like to concentrate on the Sumerian Tablets because the archaeology can be seen by many people in order to be corroborated. This is also why I do not like to talk about other alien beings such as the Reptilians, Blue Avians, Arcturans, Sirians, Pleiadians, Nordics, and so forth. Many of these beings are said to exist by abductees, but not to the extent of the Greys. The Greys overwhelmingly dominate the bulk of any abductee case. I am one that actually thinks that the beings that some have called the Sirians, Pleiadians, Nordics, and Tall Whites, are all the Anunnaki since they are all human looking; or should I say that 'we' look like they do.

If you doubt the truthfulness of all the abductees, not just a percentage, but all of them, then think of what we humans do to other animal species. If a bear needs to be relocated to another geographical location, what do we do? If you are the bear, you are going about your business eating honey, salmon and scratching your back on trees when all of a sudden you here a strange noise. You look up to see where it is coming from and you see a craft of some sort that you do not recognize (helicopter). Frightened, you try to run away as it the craft descends out of the sky and closer to you. It seems to be chasing you which terrifies you more. Gaining on you, you try your best to get away but, you feel a sharp pain (tranquilizer dart) and then start to fall unconscious until you have no memory of what happened. The humans tag the animal (implant if necessary), take the animal on board the craft or put it on another vehicle (truck) that arrives shortly. The bear is relocated to another location and then left at a place where it will awake safely. Once the bear awakes, it has no memory of what happened except that it had gone through a stressful unknown situation. Indeed, if the bear could talk and would try to talk to other bears about its ordeal, the other bears would think it is crazy or not understand at all. Is this such a far-off, unbelievable thing that could happen to anyone of us, IF there really is a technologically superior species that monitors our planet? In fact, I believe that we are just now reaching a point in our technological advancement in order to try to understand and make sense of some of the things people witness.

In 1942 if I told you that radar waves exist all around us that we could not hear, see, feel, smell, or sense in anyway, you would think that I am utterly insane. Just a few years later, however, nobody could doubt that radar waves did exist all around us. We just had to reach a certain level of technological advancement in order to assemble a machine that could detect them.

Getting back to when we can expect the Anunnaki's return, Sir Isaac Newton (1643 – 1727) as well as Johannes Kepler spent a fair amount of time trying to make sense of the Star of Bethlehem. They believed that the star was not a star at all but, a celestial alignment. (Or perhaps it was the planet Nibiru) The Jews were forbidden to use astrology to foretell upcoming events and would not understand. This is why the 3 Magi could navigate the event and follow it to where Jesus was born. The Magi were Sumerians (Chaldeans), most likely to be Persian Zoroastrians to be exact. Newton contributed largely to the principles of physics that we use today. Newton was a Christian, but would be deemed a heretic in those time standards as well as todays. He looked at the Bible with a literal interpretation and by researching prophecy in the book of Daniel and the book of Revelation in the Bible, he published that he thought the Apocalypse would take place in the year 2060 a.d. Newton wrote an unpublished treatise which was a guide for literal interpretation of the Bible called "Rules for interpreting the words & language in scripture." Newton looked at the reign of the Antichrist in Revelation which he determined to be 1,260 years. He took the word "days" spoken of in Revelation to be mistranslated to mean "years." Following the rise of the papacy in Rome he determined that the start of the countdown of 1,260 years began in 800 a.d. with the crowning of Charlemagne. So, his determination was the year 2060 a.d.

This date of Newton's (2060 a.d.) is very close to a year of Jubilee in 2067 a.d. and just 100 years off of my theorized date from the possible time of the Exodus (1433 b.c.) and the return of 2167 a.d. Newton stressed that this date was not certain and said that the wicked would not understand when the end times were anyway.

This brings us up to where I am today. Still searching and frustrated that I can't pinpoint for certain the identities of God and Satan and Jesus. I have hunches, but still trying to make sense of which side is the "good" side and which side is the "bad" side. Of course, we would all probably would want to be on the "good" side, however, it is not clear which side that is. God in the Bible is an amalgamation of the Anunnaki mostly being Enki who could also be the devil, the serpent, and Satan. Enlil too could possibly be one or the other. Both had attributes that corresponded to God and to Satan when cross referenced with the Bible. Enlil was not promiscuous and kept his fidelity with his wife, whereas Enki was very promiscuous and did not seem to have a filter when it came to matters of sex, just like Satanists are in their rituals today. Yet, Enki is the one who was the God of Abraham, Isaac, Jacob, and Moses. This tidbit of information is in the Sumerian Tablets and I feel it is certain when cross referencing with the Bible. I believe anyone would come to this conclusion if they researched it themselves. Whether Enki was the God of Samson, Saul, David, and Solomon is unclear. Also, it seems that the identity of Jesus Christ is also unclear because it is unknown to which God (Anunnaki) he was referring to when he spoke.

One thing I do know for certain. It is that the Abrahamic faiths and many religions of different civilizations throughout history are all based on the Anunnaki. I believe in 100 years or more, this fact will be better known and more accepted. For all truth passes through three stages, as stated by Arthur Schopenhauer (1788 – 1860), a famous German philosopher:

1) First, it is ridiculed.

2) Second, it is violently opposed.

3) Third, it is accepted as being self-evident.

I would encourage readers to continue to read any authors of the Sumerian Tablets or to look up the translations on Oxford University's official website. ETCSL

I also think the best place to start are the books of Zechariah Sitchin (1920 – 2010). I suggest a certain order of his books that would help the reader in a chronological order if one is a Christian or Jew and knows the Bible well. I would start with "The Lost Book of Enki: Memoirs and Prophecies of an Extraterrestrial God." Then I recommend, "Genesis Revisited." I then would proceed to the 7-book series, "The Earth Chronicles." If you were as interested as I was in his books, I recommend you read all 14, as well as, the works of Alessandro Demontis, the books of Mauro Biglino, Dr. George Smith, Gerald Clark, Dr. Sasha Alex-Lessin, ect. There are many others that are discovering this and publishing their books, but for now, the main population of this planet is in the dark about it.

Even if you don't want to accept this premise, I urge you to go back and read your Bibles. With the knowledge learned from this book and the authors above, you will now read scripture in a new light that you have not done before. One day everyone will know the truth about the Anunnaki and we will await that day when THEY return.

Epilogue

There is no doubt that the God of Abraham, Isaac, Jacob, and Moses was Enki of the Anunnaki. He was the serpent in the Garden of Eden. Throughout the Sumerian Tablets he was the one that was benevolent to mankind when his half-brother Enlil wanted mankind destroyed. Whether the God of Samson, Saul, David and Solomon was Enki as well, or one of the other Anunnaki, is not clear. When Enki spoke to Moses on Mt. Sinai, it is also not clear if he was doing so under the orders of Enlil or acting alone. Remember that Enlil was heir to the throne and outranked Enki by blood-rite, even if their father, Anu, tended to side with Enki on most occasions when a disagreement appeared between the two half-brothers. The Bible is like the last chapter that still exists of the story of the Anunnaki, but only from the perspective of the side of the Enkiites.

Pinpointing the identity of Satan and Jesus is also not definite. One thing is for sure and that is they are all of the Anunnaki. Zecharia Sitchin also had trouble trying to identifiy the God of Abraham. He thought that none of the Anunnaki fit exactly, so he went to a default and stated that the being above the Anunnaki that they called "The Creator" must be God. That makes sense in the Jewish and Christian tradition with the Anunnaki all being angels, but none of them as God. However, "The Creator" was never mentioned or even alluded to having or wanting a worship of him in any form. He did not need temples or rules and laws that he handed down. The Anunnaki did. "The Creator" was only mentioned twice in the 100,000's of cuneiform tablets that have been recovered and even those were brief and vague.

Some authors and researchers have subscribed to the notion that King Anu has abdicated his throne not to his sons Enlil or Enki; not to his grandsons Ninurta, or Marduk, but to his grandson Nannar (Allah) who was arguably fifth in line for the crown. We have no writings that this is so. The subscription to this idea comes directly from a "channeler", Wes Penre, who has gained quite a following. Penre goes on to talk about a galactic federation of different species that hold and govern territory of space throughout the galaxy much like Gene Rodenberry's, Star Trek. Even if this is true, we have no written records of it so I cannot accept it as if it were written in the archaeology. This Galactic Federation is also being described and accepted by government whistleblowers with possible knowledge to classified information. Paul Hellyer is probably the highest-ranking politician to go on record that this is true. Hellyer was involved with Canadian politics for 20 years. Paul Hellyer once held the position of Canada's Minister of Defense (April 1963 – Sept. 1967). Regardless of this information, I have chosen only to talk about what has been written in the archaeology. If this Galactic Federation is true, where do the Anunnaki rank within the organization?

What is true is that "crumbs" are being exposed from top secret classified information on UFO's and the existence of extraterrestrials. A search for British citizen, Gary McKinnon, will provide some information that he talked about before signing a non-disclosure agreement. McKinnon illegally infiltrated NASA and Pentagon databases for many years in the 90's. He said he saw about 30 names with rank that were described as Non-terrestrial officers and that the U.S. has a classified space fleet. The U.S. government tried for many years to get him extradited to America to stand trial. The U.S. finally dropped the case given that McKinnon must follow certain rules if he were to remain free.

Hopefully, the future will bring new discoveries and more cuneiform tablets unearthed that will be another piece of the puzzle that is missing. There is no doubt that mankind was created by the Anunnaki with fighting going on among themselves. Maybe one day we will know who created our creators. Until that day comes, if it comes before the final battle of the Anunnaki, I will keep searching.

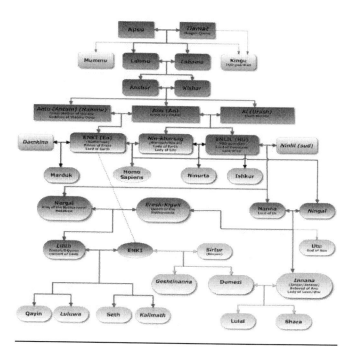

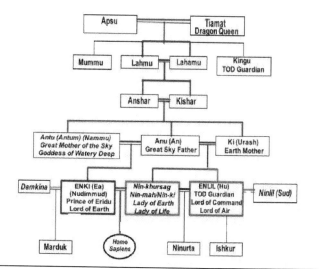

Bibliography

1. Smith, George "*The Chaldean Account of Genesis*" Babylonian Fables, and Legends of the Gods (1876)

2. "*Holy Bible*" English Standard Version (ESV) Value Compact Edition (2005)

3. "*Holy Bible*" Heirloom Family Bible, King James Version (KJV) (1988)

4. "*The Oxford Annotated Bible with The Apocrypha*" Revised Standard Version (RSV) College Edition (1965)

5. "*The Book of Enoch*" second edition compiled and edited by Brown, Ronald K., D. Div., Ph.D., P.E. Guadalupe Baptist Theological Seminary (1997)

6. "*Apocrypha*" Authorized King James Version (KJV) (1992)

7. Jacobs, Alan "*The Essential Gnostic Gospels*" (2009)

8. Lumpkin, Joseph "*The Book of Giants*" The Watchers, Nephilim, and the Book of Enoch (2014)

9. "*The Book of Mormon*" Another Testament of Jesus Christ (1981) originally in 1830.

10. "*The Kolbrin Bible*" 21st Century Master Edition (2005)

11. "*The Qur'an*" Translation in English by Abdullah, Yusuf Ali, Sixth U.S. Edition (2001)

12. "*The Vengeful Djinn*" Unveiling the hidden agendas of Genies, Guiley, Rosemary Ellen and Imbrogno, Philip J. (2011)

13. "*The Emerald Tablets of Thoth-The-Atlantean*" Translation and Interpretation by DOREAL, M. Dr. of the Brotherhood of the White Temple (1996)

14. Clark, Gerald MSEE, PSI, "*The Anunnaki of Nibiru*" Mankind's forgotten creators, enslavers, destroyers, saviors, and hidden architects of the New World Order (2015)

15. Fowler, Raymond E. "*The Watchers*" The Secret Design Behind UFO Abduction (1990)

16. Fowler, Raymond E. "*The Watchers II*" Exploring UFO's and the Near-Death Experience (1995)

17. Corso, Philip J. Colonel (ret.) with Birnes, William J. "*The Day After Roswell*" (1997)

18. Birnes, William J., The UFO Magazine "_UFO Encyclopedia_" (2004)

19. Sitchin, Zechariah "_The Lost Book of Enki_" Memoirs and Prophecies of an Extraterrestrial God (2002)

20. Sitchin, Zechariah "_Genesis Revisited_" Is Modern Science Catching up with Ancient Knowledge? (1990)

21. Sitchin, Zechariah "_The 12th Planet_" The First Book of The Earth Chronicles (1976)

22. Sitchin, Zechariah "_The Stairway to Heaven_" The Second Book of The Earth Chronicles (1980)

23. Sitchin, Zechariah "_The Wars of Gods and Men_" The Third Book of The Earth Chronicles (1990)

24. Sitchin, Zechariah "_The Lost Realms_" The Fourth Book of The Earth Chronicles (1990)

25. Sitchin, Zechariah "_When Time Began_" The Fifth Book of The Earth Chronicles (1993)

26. Sitchin, Zechariah "_The Cosmic Code_" The Sixth Book of The Earth Chronicles (1998)

27. Sitchin, Zechariah "_The End of Days_" Armageddon and Prophecies of the Return,

The Seventh Book of The Earth Chronicles (2007)

28. Sitchin, Zecharia "*Divine Encounters*" A Guide to Visions, Angels, and Other Emissaries (1995)

29. Sitchin, Zecharia "*The Earth Chronicles Handbook*" A Comprehensive Guide to the Seven Books of The Earth Chronicles (2009)

30. Sitchin, Zecharia "*Journeys to the Mythical Past*" (2009)

31. Sitchin, Zechariah "*There Were Giants Upon the Earth*" Gods, Demigods, and Human Ancestry: The Evidence of Alien DNA (2010 copyright) first published (2016)

32. Sitchin, Zechariah "*The Earth Chronicles Expeditions*" (2007)

33. Sitchin, Zechariah "*The King Who Refused to Die*" The Anunnaki and the Search for Immortality (2013 from the estate of Zechariah Sitchin)

34. "*The Anunnaki Chronicles*" A Zechariah Sitchin Reader, Includes Never Before Published Writings, Edited by Janet Sitchin (2015)

35. Masters, Phil "*The Wars of Atlantis*" (2015)

36.   Childress, David Hatcher and Foerster, Brien "*The Enigma of Cranial Deformation*" Elongated Skulls of the Ancients (2012)

37.   Foerster, Brien "*Elongated Skulls of Peru and Bolivia: The Path of Viracocha*" (2015)

38.   Levay, Anton "*The Satanic Bible*" (1969)

39.   "*The Tibetan Book of the Dead*" First Complete Translation (2006)

40.   Pagels, Elaine "*The Gnostic Gospels*" (1979)

41.   Budge, E.A. Wallis and Willis, Epiphanius A.M "*The Ancient Egyptian Book of the Dead*" (2018)

42.   Hancock, Graham "Magicians of the Gods": The Forgotten Wisdom of Earth's Lost Civilizations (2015)

Made in the USA
San Bernardino, CA
18 June 2019